How To...

Enjoy Guitar With Just Three Chords

Including Songs by: Bob Dylan • Weezer • The Beatles
Bob Marley • Nirvana and Many More!

by David Harrison

ISBN 978-1-5400-4599-7

HAL•LEONARD®

Visit Hal Leonard Online at
www.halleonard.com

Contact us:
Hal Leonard
7777 West Bluemound Road
Milwaukee, WI 53213
Email: info@halleonard.com

In Europe, contact:
Hal Leonard Europe Limited
42 Wigmore Street
Marylebone, London, W1U 2RN
Email: info@halleonardeurope.com

In Australia, contact:
Hal Leonard Australia Pty. Ltd.
4 Lentara Court
Cheltenham,   Victoria,   3192   Australia
Email: info@halleonard.com.au

CONTENTS

GETTING STARTED

Whether you're playing acoustic or electric guitar, a good posture will help save on discomfort, effort, and frustration.

Choose a chair or stool that's high enough so that your feet are flat on the ground but your back doesn't slump. Keep your shoulders even and slightly back for a straight, stable sitting position.

Beginning guitarists are often very tempted to peek over to see the front of the guitar—or else to tilt the guitar back—to see what the hands are doing. This can make you feel cramped and tense, so get used to checking that you're sitting in a relaxed, comfortable position with the guitar facing forward. As you progress, you'll start to feel your hands getting into position quite naturally without constantly having to check how it looks.

Whatever kind of guitar you play, it'll have the same few basic parts—so let's take a look.

TUNING PEGS

Located on the *headstock*, these tighten or loosen the strings to tune the guitar.

FRETS

The neck is divided into sections called *frets*, which are separated by short wires running across the neck called *fretwires*. You'll place your left-hand fingers in the space just behind the fretwires to create different notes. The entire surface of the neck is called the *fretboard* or *fingerboard*. Each fret is given a number starting with the one nearest the headstock. Your guitar may have fret markers to help you count the frets. In this book however, you'll only be using the first three frets.

STRINGS

The strings are numbered from 1 to 6, starting with the thinnest.

LEFT HAND

Your left hand should be placed around the guitar neck as shown in the photo. Place the pad of your thumb gently behind the neck. This will help to support the guitar, and you'll find that your fingers have plenty of room to move into position on the fretboard.

Many guitarists wrap their thumbs right around the neck, gripping it tightly, but if you're aiming for maximum comfort and reach, the hand position shown here will give you both. Notice that there's a gap between the bottom of the neck and the hand; the back of the hand is reasonably straight, keeping the fingers out in front.

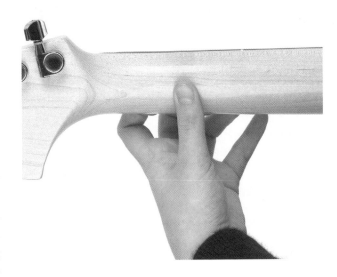

RIGHT HAND

The right hand strums the strings (brushing across several strings to create a rhythmic accompaniment). Some guitarists like to use a pick, but for simple strumming the thumb and fingers will do just fine.

With the right forearm loosely resting over the top of the guitar body, let the right hand hang gently over the strings. Ideally, you should be able to follow a continuous curve starting at your right shoulder, through the elbow and down to the wrist, ending with the hand. Keep everything relaxed to avoid tension and discomfort.

Try strumming down across the strings with your thumb. It shouldn't take much effort. If you have a strong thumbnail you can use this; it'll give you a slightly crisper sound. Once you've strummed across the strings, return the hand to its starting position.

FINGERS

We also number the fingers of the left hand which will help in creating the chord shapes.

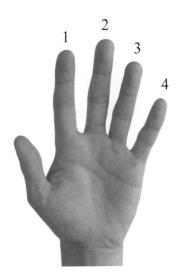

UNDERSTANDING CHORD SHAPES

Every song in this book can be played using just three chords. In fact, there are thousands of other songs that use nothing but these chords too. Once you've mastered them, you'll be well on your way to playing the guitar!

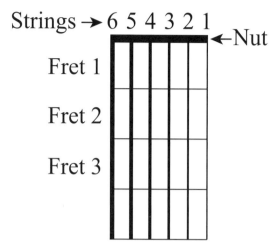

Chords are shown using a special grid called a chord diagram, with strings drawn as vertical lines and frets as horizontal lines. The *nut* at the top of the neck is shown as a thicker vertical line. Although it might seem strange to look at chords as though you were holding the guitar upright, you'll soon get used to it. This is how chord shapes are drawn in songbooks and sheet music.

Notice how the strings are arranged in order of thickness just as they are on a real guitar, with the 6th string on the far left. **The thickest string (the 6th string) is also known as the "bottom string" since it creates the lowest sound, while the thinnest (the 1st string) is also called the "top string" because it sounds highest.**

In standard chord diagrams you won't usually see the strings drawn in different thicknesses, but it's quite useful for now. In addition, fretted strings (those with fingers on them) are shown with a black spot where a finger should be positioned. The number below indicates which finger is to be used.

In this example, three fingers are placed on the strings while two other strings are played *open* (that is, without any fingers on them). An open string is indicated by the "o" above the string. Notice the "x" placed over the bottom string. This shows that the 6th string shouldn't be played at all. We'll see this same chord diagram again in a moment and it'll probably be a bit clearer when you see it together with a photo of the same chord being played.

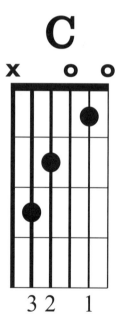

You'll need to use three fingers for each of the chords in this book. To avoid your fingers getting in the way of each other and to create a clean, clear sound, ensure that the fingertips are placed precisely on the string just behind the correct fretwire. This is a lot easier to achieve if you spend a little time checking that your overall left-hand position is comfortable and not cramped up, with the thumb placed on the back of the neck. Allow the fingers plenty of room to come down onto the strings more or less at right angles to the fingerboard.

If you're struggling to position your fingers accurately, go back and look through the section on left-hand position (page 5).

THE THREE CHORDS

THE C CHORD

Here's that same chord, but now with a photo to help you make more sense of the chord diagram. Your first finger (the index finger) is positioned on the 1st fret of the 2nd string, with your second finger (the middle finger) on the 2nd fret of the 4th string. Finally, you'll need your third finger (the ring finger) on the 3rd fret of the 5th string. When you have all the fingers in position, try brushing your right thumb down across the strings to hear how it sounds.

Try placing each finger one at a time until you get used to the feel of it. Once it starts to feel familiar, try lifting the fingers off and putting them back down *all at the same time*. This is how you'll eventually learn to change chord shapes swiftly and smoothly. It'll take a little while, so don't be in a rush to perfect this skill; it'll soon begin to feel easier.

As you brush across the strings with your right thumb, try to listen for any dull-sounding strings and adjust the angle at which your left-hand fingers contact the string if necessary. You'll rarely find you have to press hard—accurate placement is much more important. Be prepared for it to sound a bit muffled at the beginning, but if you form good habits, your sound will soon improve.

THE G CHORD

The second chord, G, uses all six strings. Some people find this chord to be a bit of a stretch at the start, so let's begin with a simpler version of the shape that uses just the top four strings. You'll need a finger on the 3rd fret of the 1st string, as shown in the diagram. Use either the third or fourth finger. When you tackle the full chord shape, you'll see why. Ideally, when you play this version of the chord, you won't strum the lower two strings (the thickest ones).

This shape will give you a good idea of the way a G chord should sound, but for the full effect, it's time to take a look at the six-string shape. There are two main ways of fingering this shape: either using your first finger as shown in the first photo, or else as shown in the second photo, without the first finger.

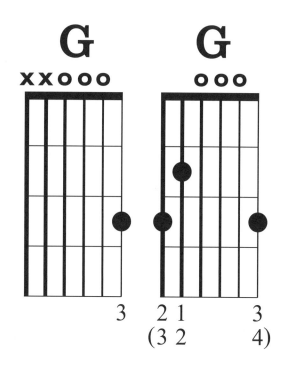

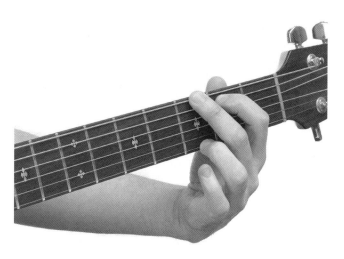

Notice in the first photo that the third finger is used on the top string, while in the second photo the little finger takes its place. It's really a question of what feels most comfortable, although the second version will eventually be a more useful shape to move smoothly to and from other chord shapes, even if it doesn't feel quite so natural to start with.

Try changing from the C shape we've already looked at and you'll see that when using the G chord shown in the second photo, the second and third fingers simply have to move across a single string; whereas in the first version you'll need to entirely reposition your fingers.

Practice moving your fingers into position together. Soon you'll think of the overall shape instead of individual finger positions. Whichever of the two fingering options you choose for the full G shape, be prepared to spend a bit of time getting the 5th string to sound clearly; you'll need to check that it isn't being muffled by the finger on the 6th string. Stick with it, keep checking your overall hand position, and it'll soon start to sound crisp and full.

THE D CHORD

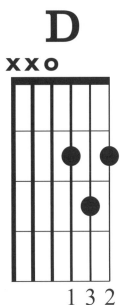

The final chord we'll need is D, which only uses four strings. Notice how the fingers in the photo are coming pretty much straight down onto the strings. With the thumb pad placed at the back of the neck, the fingers have room to get into position without being cramped.

Start by placing the first finger on the 2nd fret of the 3rd string and it should be quite easy to position the other two fingers. As before, practice removing the fingers together and putting them all back on together. Take it slowly at first until you build up enough muscle memory for the fingers to find their own way.

The bottom two strings aren't played in this shape. The open 4th string is itself tuned to the note D, and that's the lowest D on the guitar. When the lowest note in a chord is the note for which the chord is named, it helps the chord to sound solid or musically grounded. Take a look at the C chord shape we've looked at and the previous full G shape. In each case, the bottom note (3rd fret of the 5th string for C, 3rd fret of the 6th string for G) is the note for which the chord is named.

READING THE SONGS

Okay, that's all three chords—so we're almost ready to make some music! Let's just take a moment to look at the way the songs in this book are laid out. Here are some tips and tricks to help you make the most of them.

BEATS AND BARS

Music is written out in a linear fashion from left to right, just like ordinary text but with extra info to let you know what to play… and crucially, *when* to play it. In music, rhythmic symbols are used to show how the music works over time, and in this book the basic rhythmic unit (the *beat*) is indicated with *rhythm slashes*.

Take a look at the following example in which the beats are arranged in repeating groups. You'll see the *count* above each rhythm slash. In this example, the groups of beats, called *measures* or *bars*, are four beats long. All the songs in this book have four-beat measures. Four beats to the bar is very common in pop or rock, but in other styles you'll often find measures of different lengths. For example, marches are generally two beats to the bar (think "left-right, left-right"), while a waltz is three beats to the bar (as in "oom-pah-pah, oom-pah-pah").

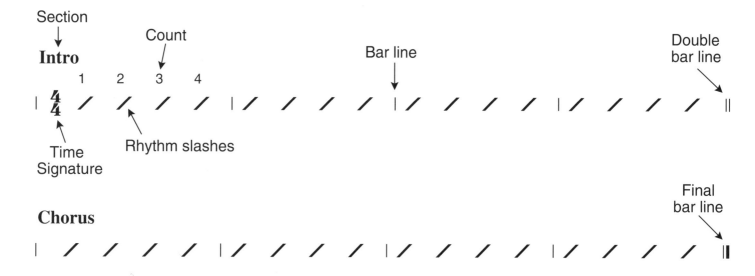

Generally, the first beat of the measure is emphasized. This might mean that it's played more loudly (with an *accent*) or it might just be "felt" that way. But once you start to play, you'll get a sense of the way the measures help create a natural flow to the music. If you were going to play one chord per measure, you'd ideally strum the chord on the first beat and then leave it ringing throughout the remainder of the measure.

By the way, you'll see two "4"s placed one above the other at the beginning of the music. This is the *time signature* and simply means that in this piece there are four beats to each measure, so you'll always have four rhythm slashes in each.

BAR LINES

The measures are separated by vertical dividers called *bar lines*. A pair of bar lines written together, known as a *double bar line*, is used to indicate the end of a section of music; and at the very end of a piece of music you'll see a *final bar line* made up of a standard single bar line followed by a thicker one.

SECTIONS

The various parts of the songs are indicated too: intro, verse, chorus, and so on. There are also special symbols to show when a part should be repeated and even to show when repeated sections end differently, but we'll look at all of that later. For now, get used to the idea of counting four regular beats in each measure, and (assuming you know the song you're learning) the lyrics should also help you to keep your place.

CHANGING FROM CHORD TO CHORD

Moving swiftly and confidently from one chord shape to the next is one of the keys to playing smoothly and in time on the guitar. Although all three shapes we're using look completely different from one another, there are a few similarities.

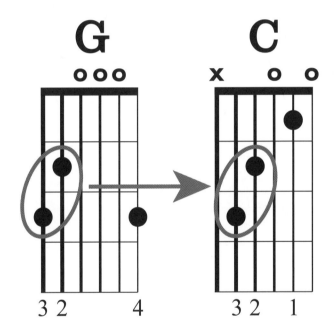

Rather than entirely moving your hand to reposition the fingers every time you form a new shape, take a look to see what elements of the previous chord you can use. For example, try moving between G and C. If you're playing the six-string version of the G chord, you'll notice that the two fingers on the 5th and 6th strings are placed in exactly the same relationship to each other as when they're on the 4th and 5th strings of a C chord. Simply move the second and third fingers together across to the correct strings. One more tweak and you're playing the next chord! Look back at the two fingerings for the full G shape on page 8 and you'll see why the second version is useful.

It might not seem quite so obvious when moving between G and D, but you can make use of certain features here too. For example, when you're fingering the D chord shape, the little finger is hanging around doing nothing. Just as you move the fingers away from the D shape, move the little finger into position (up on the 3rd fret of the 1st string) and before you know it, you're well on your way to forming the G shape.

When moving between C and D, there isn't a lot to cling onto that's going to help you transition to the new shape. In each case, try getting the first finger into position first: for the C chord it's on the 2nd string, and for the D chord it's on the 3rd string. If at least that much becomes automatic, you'll find that the other fingers will start to fall obediently in line.

Changing from chord to chord does require a bit of practice, but there's no need to completely abandon one shape before starting to form the next. Eventually, you'll "feel" each chord shape with your fingers as an interconnected series of movements, rather than individual and separate finger positions.

For now, as you change chords within the songs, clearly strum the chord once on the first beat of the measure. Use the remaining beats to get your fingers into position for the next chord. Your aim should always be to play the new chord at the beginning of the next measure. You'll start to get a sense for how long you can keep hold of a chord and how much time you'll need to get to the new one. Above all, practice slowly at first and make controlled, deliberate movements until you start to build up muscle memory.

BARBARA ANN

For our first song, this Beach Boys classic from 1965, you've got plenty of time to stay on each chord.

You'll primarily be switching between G and C, with a single measure of D toward the end of the chorus. Listen to the original recording of the song if you're not familiar with it and try to get a sense of the *form* of the song (how the song sections are organized). If you manage to memorize parts of the chord sequence, you won't need to keep your eyes glued to the page and you'll be free to monitor your left hand as it changes chords.

Strum down across the strings at the beginning of each measure, letting the chord ring on for the remainder of the beats. Remember to start preparing your hand to move to the new shape in good time. This will soon become more fluid.

Notice that the first four measures use nothing but a G chord, so the chord name is only written above the first measure. The first measure of the following section, the chorus, also begins on the G chord.

Intro

G

| / / / / | / / / / |

(Ba,   Ba,   Ba,   Ba,   Bar - b'ra Ann.

| / / / / | / / / / ||

Ba,   Ba,   Ba,   Ba,   Bar - b'ra Ann.)   Bar - b'ra

Chorus

G

| / / / / | / / / / |

Ann,   take   my

(Ba,   Ba,   Ba,   Ba,   Bar - b'ra Ann.

C

| / / / / | / / / / |

hand.   Ba - b'ra

Ba,   Ba,   Ba,   Ba,   Bar - b'ra Ann.

G

| / / / / | / / / / |

Ann,   you got me

Ba,   Ba,   Ba,   Ba,   Bar - b'ra Ann.)

D   C

| / / / / | / / / / |

rock - in' and a roll - in', rock - in' and a reel - in', Bar - b'ra

STARTING TO STRUM

One of the main right-hand techniques is *strumming*: brushing across the strings in a rhythmic fashion. Generally, you'll want to play a repeating rhythm (also known as a *strumming pattern*) that continues throughout a section or even for a whole song.

STRUMMING BASICS

Let's start by strumming down across the strings. Aim for a relaxed arm, especially at the wrist. Ideally, the wrist is where most of the hand movement will come from. You might be tempted to swing from the elbow, but a fluid strumming technique comes from a flexible wrist. Move the right hand down across the strings over the sound hole (or the general area over the pickups on an electric guitar), brushing the strings with the backs of your fingernails. You'll probably find that just a couple of fingers naturally make contact with the strings—maybe the first and second fingers, or perhaps the second and third—which is perfect.

Aim for a steady, regular feel, keep the fingers loose, and experiment with different speeds and pressure; you shouldn't need to brush too hard. Once the hand has strummed down across all the strings, move the hand back up and start again. Strumming down once on each beat while counting is a great first step to establishing a reliable, comfortable accompaniment technique. In songs containing four beats per measure this will produce quarter notes.

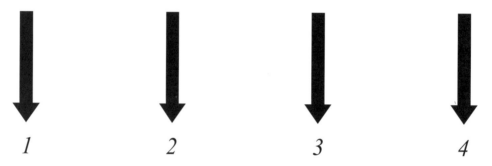

Remember, rotate the wrist to lift the hand up and then slowly strum back down. Keep the movements subtle and flowing, and once you have a feel for it, move on to a pattern like the one below. Here we're strumming lightly on beats 1 and 3 and more firmly on beats 2 and 4. This creates the impression of a *backbeat*, which is what the drummer often plays in pop and rock. Try counting "1, *2*, 3, *4*" as you strum. You might find the lighter strums sound great on just the lower (thicker) strings, with the firmer strums played on the higher (thinner) strings for contrast. Aim for an even, flowing beat.

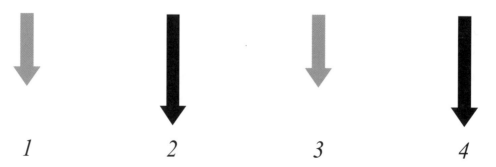

The next song, Nirvana's "All Apologies," is perfect for practicing this strumming pattern. As before, take it slowly at first and try getting an overview of the structure of the song so that you're able to think about what's coming up next, rather than just reading measure by measure from the page.

ALL APOLOGIES

Here's a simple Nirvana song to play using the first pattern we looked at.

Notice that the entire verse is on a single chord, G. This should give you plenty of time to get into the pattern. Listen to the original recording for inspiration and you'll be able to hear the backbeat mentioned on page 16. Keep the strums steady and consistent for a solid rock feel.

One more thing: at the start of the verse, there's a double bar line followed by a pair of dots; and right at the end of the chorus, there's a mirror image of this symbol. These are a set of *repeat bar lines* (or simply, *repeats*). All the music between these repeats is played twice. So after the intro, play the verse, then the chorus, and then come back up to the verse and play it again (singing the second set of lyrics), ending with a final second chorus.

Intro

G

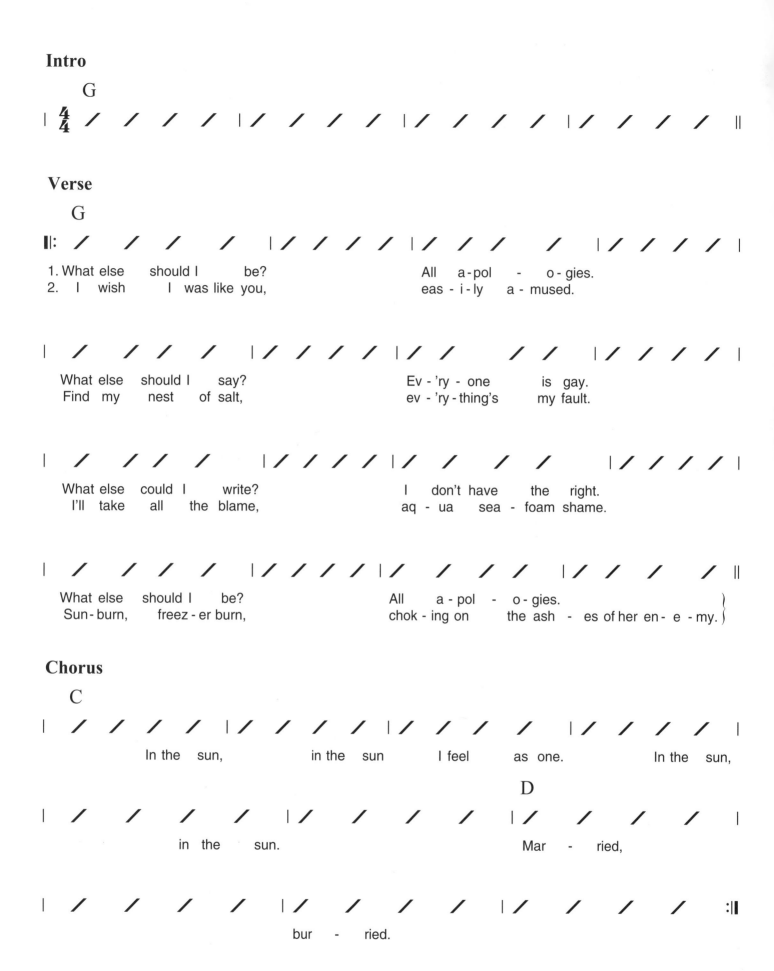

Verse

G

1. What else should I be?   All a-pol - o - gies.
2. I wish   I was like you,   eas - i - ly a - mused.

What else should I say?   Ev - 'ry - one   is gay.
Find my   nest of salt,   ev - 'ry - thing's   my fault.

What else could I write?   I don't have   the right.
I'll take   all   the blame,   aq - ua   sea - foam shame.

What else should I be?   All   a - pol - o - gies.
Sun - burn,   freez - er burn,   chok - ing on   the ash - es of her en - e - my.

Chorus

C

In the sun,   in the sun   I feel   as one.   In the sun,

D

in the sun.   Mar - ried,

bur - ried.

Words and Music by Kurt Cobain
Copyright © 1993 BMG Platinum Songs, Primary Wave Tunes and The End Of Music
All Rights Administered by BMG Rights Management (US) LLC
All Rights Reserved   Used by Permission

BEVERLY HILLS

This Weezer track has a slightly different feel. You could play our original backbeat pattern or try something custom-made for this song.

In this arrangement the guitar strums *twice* per beat, in *eighth notes* (or "half beats"). Listen to the original recording and you'll hear a strong down-strum on beat 1, followed by another strum a half of a beat later; then on beat 3 the same thing happens, which is generally when the next chord is played.

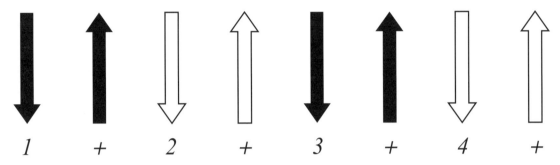

The white arrows show that you should keep your strumming hand moving up and down even when you're not making contact with the strings. This way you'll find it much easier to keep a regular rhythm going and strum accurately on the beat.

If you were counting out loud, you'd say "*one*-and-*two*-and-*three*-and-*four*-and." The "and" represents the strum in between the beats, or the *upbeat*.

Throughout the arrangement, notice the "N.C." marking every fourth measure: this stands for "no chord," meaning that you momentarily stop playing. Also, there is a new symbol over the final chord that looks like an arched line over a dot. This symbol is called a *fermata* and indicates a pause. It shows that the final chord should be held longer than usual—in this case, let the final chord ring on until it naturally dies out.

Intro

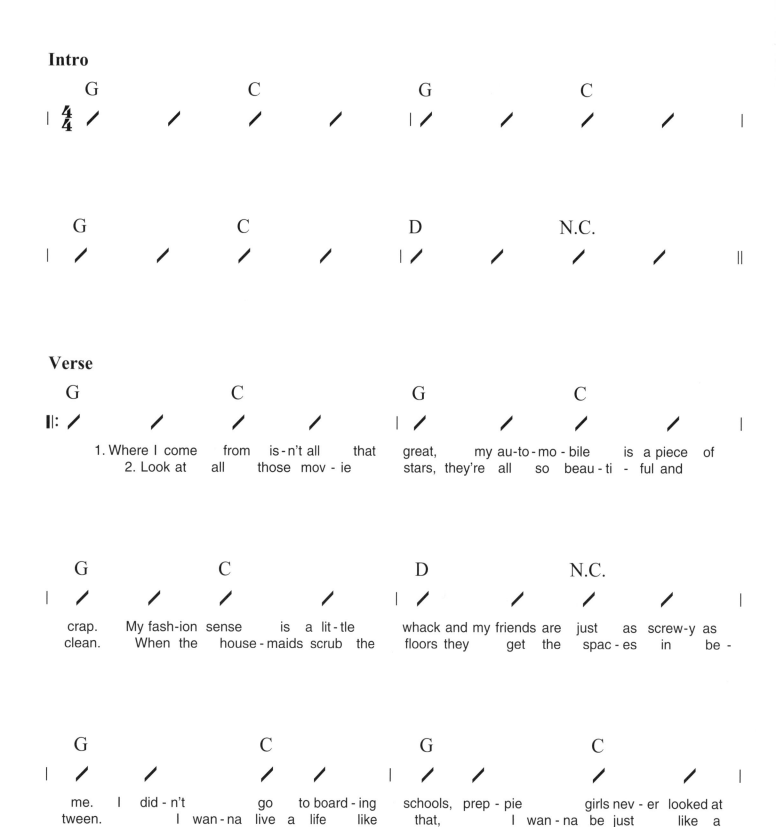

Verse

1. Where I come   from   is-n't all   that   great,   my au-to-mo-bile   is a piece of
2. Look at   all   those mov-ie   stars, they're all   so   beau-ti - ful and

crap.   My fash-ion sense   is a lit-tle   whack and my friends are   just   as   screw-y as
clean.   When the   house-maids scrub the   floors they   get the   spac-es   in   be -

me.   I did-n't   go   to board-ing   schools, prep-pie   girls nev-er   looked at
tween.   I wan-na   live a   life   like   that,   I wan-na   be just   like a

Words and Music by Rivers Cuomo
Copyright © 2005 E.O. Smith Music
All Rights Administered by Wixen Music Publishing, Inc.
International Copyright Secured   All Rights Reserved

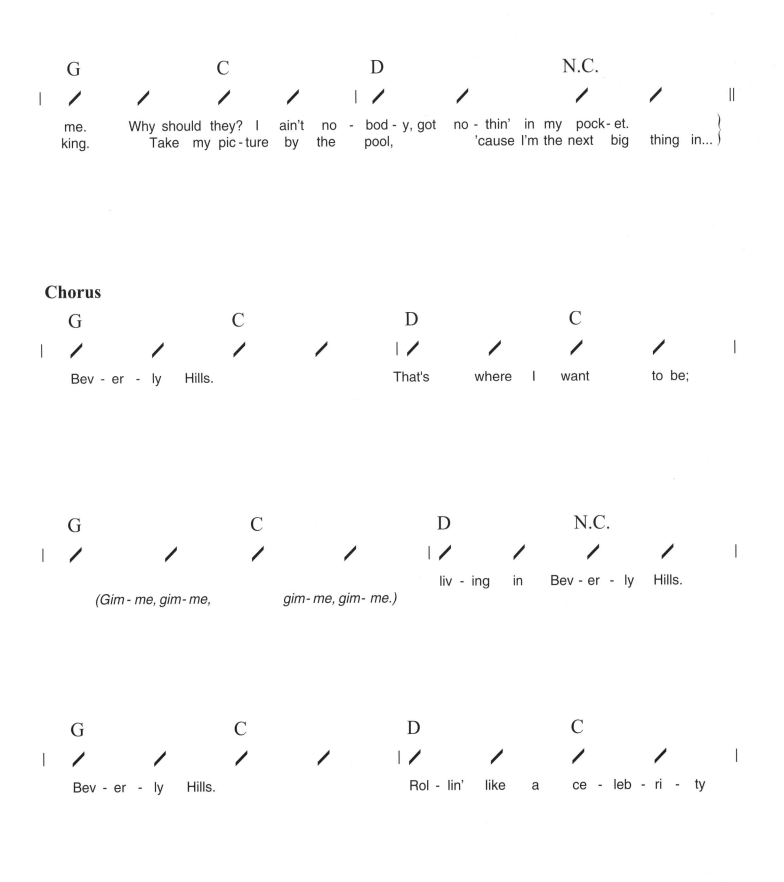

me. Why should they? I ain't no - bod - y, got no - thin' in my pock - et.

king. Take my pic - ture by the pool, 'cause I'm the next big thing in...

Chorus

G   C   D   C

Bev - er - ly Hills. That's where I want to be;

G   C   D   N.C.

(Gim - me, gim - me, gim - me, gim - me.) liv - ing in Bev - er - ly Hills.

G   C   D   C

Bev - er - ly Hills. Rol - lin' like a ce - leb - ri - ty

G   C   D   N.C.   G

(Gim - me, gim - me, gim - me, gim - me.) liv - ing in Bev - er - ly Hills.

I STILL HAVEN'T FOUND WHAT I'M LOOKING FOR

The solid, driving rhythm of this U2 classic comes from the continuous eighth-note feel of the guitar.

Practice strumming down with the backs of the fingernails and brushing the strings with the back of the thumb nail on the way back up again. Keep your wrist supple and your fingers nice and loose. It'll take a bit of trial and error to get a smooth rhythm up to speed, so start at half speed: strum down on beat 1, up on beat 2, and so on.

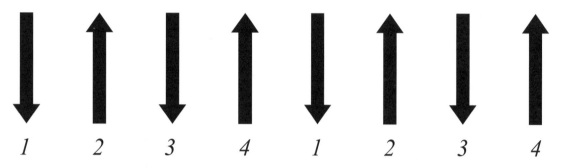

Once this feels comfortable, try doubling up by strumming down and up on every single beat to create a continuous pattern. Start slowly and build up speed gradually. You'll find it helps to strum gently and with just enough movement to keep the strumming hand in motion. Try limiting your strumming to just the top few strings for a lighter feel.

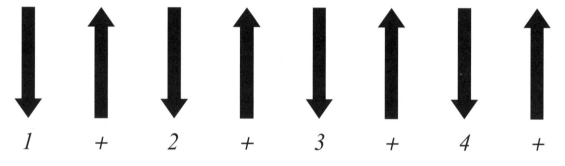

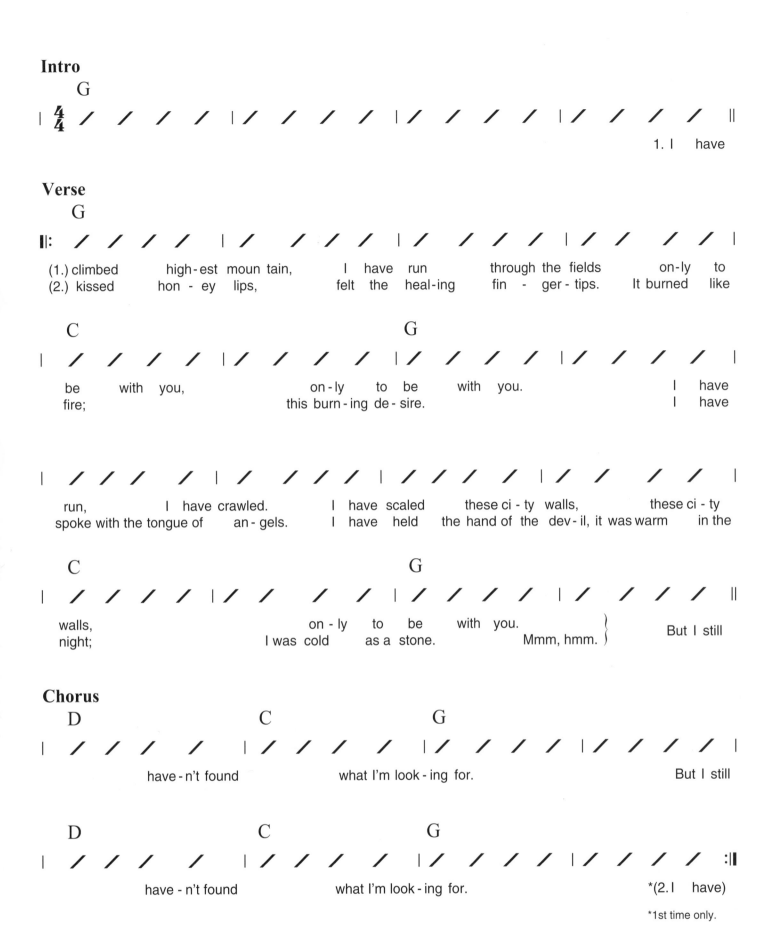

NEXT STEPS: PICKING THE BASS NOTES

Let's give our strumming style a new dimension by adding specific bass notes to the pattern.

The bass note of the chord (the 4th string for D, the 5th string for C, and—if you're playing the full shape—the 6th string for G) can be played on its own to create a more interesting accompaniment style. When picked bass notes are combined with strumming, it almost sounds as though there's more than one guitar playing!

First, a word about "bottom" and "top" (the concepts of up and down on the guitar can be a bit confusing). When we're talking about strumming, "down" really does mean down, but when we're talking about the "bottom" string, we mean the one that *sounds* lowest—although in a normal playing position this string is farthest from the ground! Conversely, the "top" string is nearest the ground. The best way to avoid confusion is just to be consistent. Where strings are concerned, we're always talking about the *sound* they create rather than their physical position; the top string is called the "top" string because it *sounds higher* than the others.

In the following diagrams, horizontal lines represent the strings as they appear in a normal playing position (so the bottom string looks highest!). The relative thicknesses of the strings are also shown just to make it a bit more obvious.

Try picking down with the thumb on the open 4th string, once on each beat. It'll take a bit of practice before you can accurately pick the chosen string at the right time without touching the other strings.

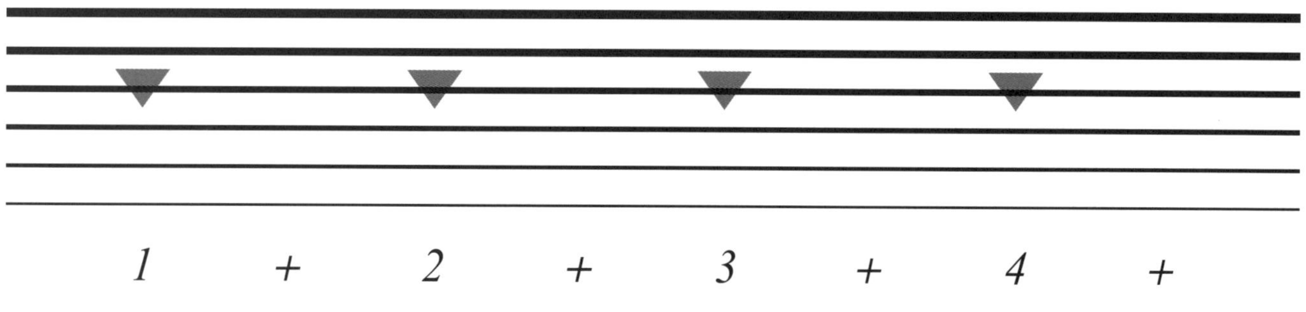

Once that's reasonably smooth, form a D chord shape and add strums on beats 2 and 4.

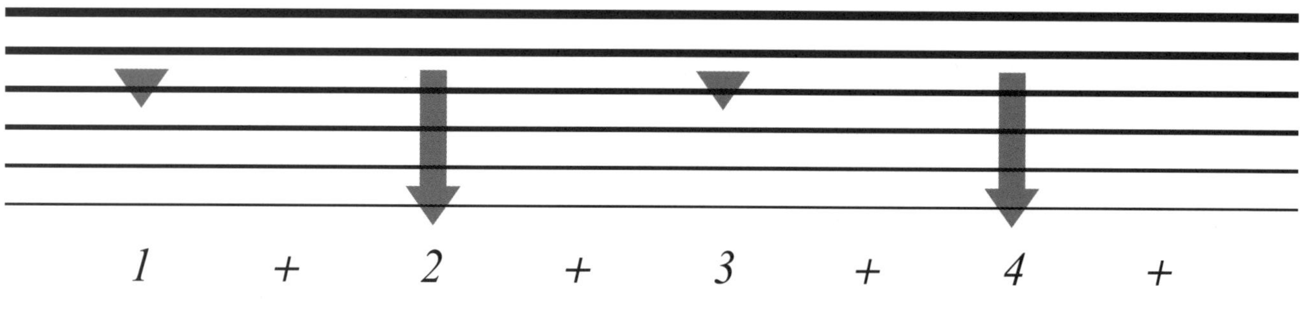

Now try the same thing for a C chord…

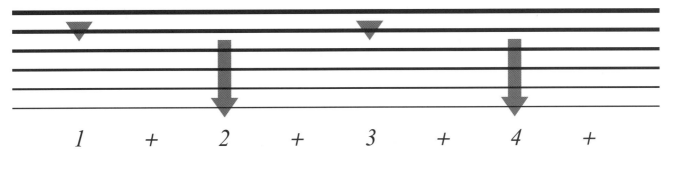

…and also, a G chord.

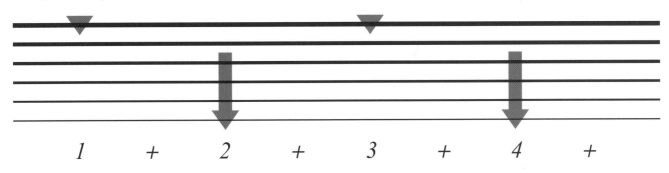

Notice that, in each case, the diagram shows the strum across the four top strings. In reality, you can include as few or as many strings above the bass note as you like. Strumming across just a few upper strings will create a greater contrast between the bass note and the strum itself.

You can also experiment with the accent (how loudly you play) for both the bass and the strum until you achieve the effect you're after. Just a little tweak can change the whole feel of the pattern.

Finally, here's a fun variation that might take a bit of time to master. Play a standard pick-strum pattern like the previous examples, but rather than using a single down-strum on beats 2 and 4, play a down-up strum on those beats instead. Here it is using a G chord with the bass notes picked on the 6th string. This rhythm creates the famous "boom, chick-a, boom, chick-a" rhythm you'll often hear in country music.

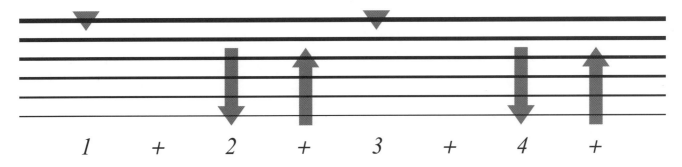

I HAVE A DREAM

This Abba number has a strong, continuous bass line. By picking individual bass notes and strumming chords in between, we can create a full-sounding accompaniment style.

You might start on this song by simply picking the correct bass note for each chord. That's the 4th string for D, the 5th string for C, and the 6th string for G. Start with a single bass note on the first beat of each measure before building up to a bass note on the first and third beats of each measure. As before, try memorizing little sections of the song.

When you're happy with your bass line, create the complete shape for each chord with the left hand and add the strumming. There's quite a lot to think about, but it'll soon become familiar and you'll do it without thinking. As with most of the songs, the repeat bar lines should help you keep an eye on the structure.

Intro

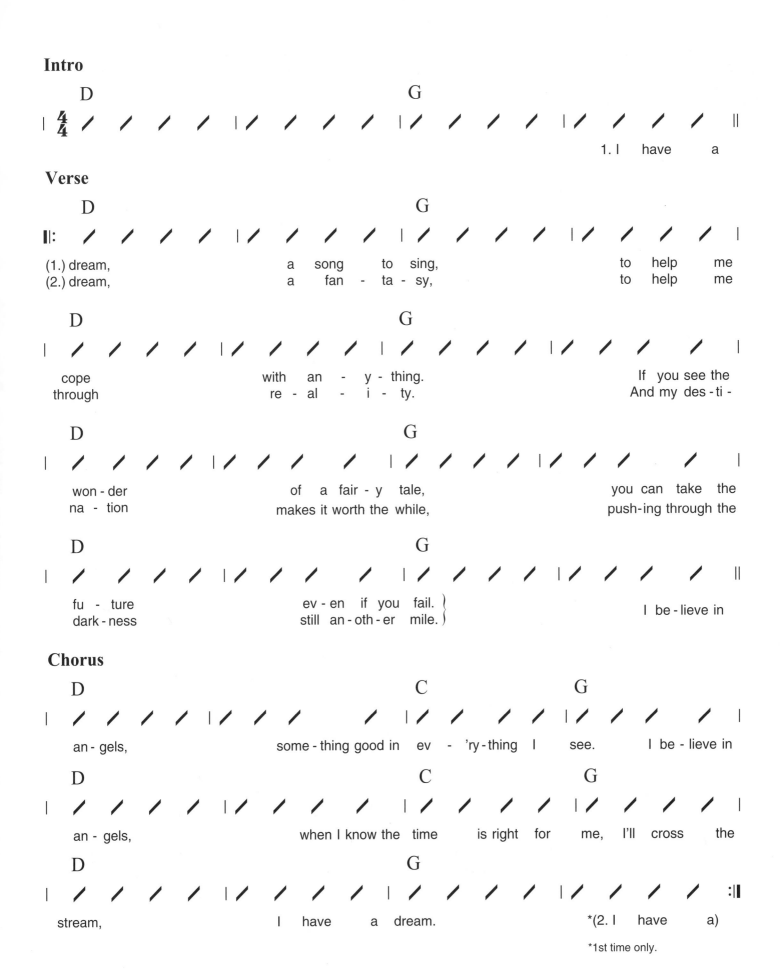

Verse

Chorus

stream, I have a dream. *(2. I have a)

*1st time only.

Words and Music by Benny Andersson and Bjorn Ulvaeus
Copyright © 1979 UNIVERSAL/UNION SONGS MUSIKFORLAG AB
All Rights in the United States and Canada Controlled and Administered by UNIVERSAL - POLYGRAM INTERNATIONAL PUBLISHING, INC.
and EMI WATERFORD MUSIC, INC.
All Rights Reserved   Used by Permission

MORE PICKING: ALTERNATING THE BASS

We're not limited to a single bass note for each chord. In some styles such as country music, changing the bass note while the chord stays the same is an established feature of the genre.

Let's begin by revisiting the D chord. We started by playing the bass note on the 4th string. That note is a D, the note after which the chord is named, so it makes perfect sense that this would be the bass note.

D

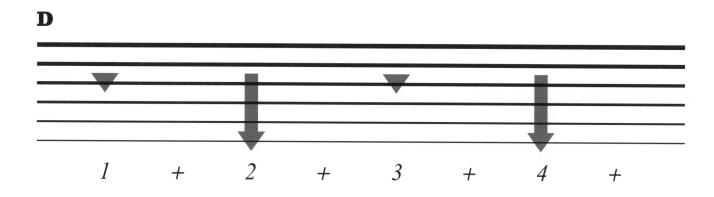

To create a bit of interest, however, it's common to move the second bass note down a string, in this case to the open 5th string.

D

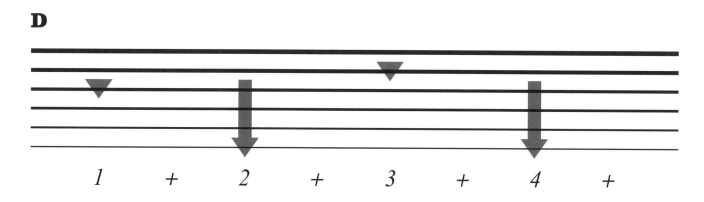

Play this over and over until the move between the 4th and 5th strings feels smooth and natural. This is such an important feature of guitar accompaniment that it is worth spending a bit of time on it. Aim for a steady, back-and-forth feel in the bass.

Once you're happy with alternating the bass on a D chord, try it with a C chord. You'll see that the bass note moves from the 5th string to the 6th string, but for this chord you'll need to make an adjustment in the left hand also. Normally, to play a C chord, the third finger is on the 3rd fret of the 5th string. But now, after you pick the 5th string, move the third finger down and place it as shown: on the 3rd fret of the 6th string.

C

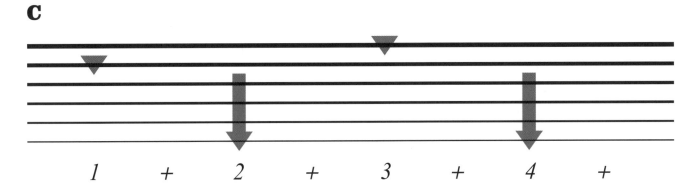

When you move the finger down to the 6th string, you'll leave the 5th string open. As long as you start your strum down on the 4th string or higher, you can avoid playing the 5th string altogether, as shown by the "x."

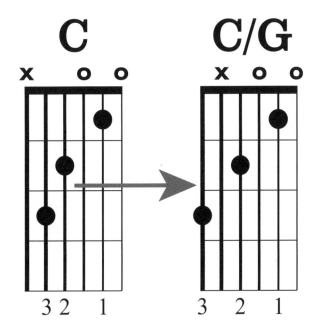

For a G chord, the alternating bass is a bit different. Since the normal bass note for G is already on the lowest string of the guitar, you won't be able to move it down a string. Instead, you'll alternate between the 6th string and the open 4th string. And the good news is, you can leave the left hand in position. Just make sure the open 4th string rings out clearly when you pick it.

G

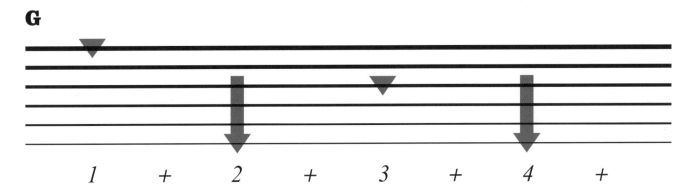

COAT OF MANY COLORS

This famous Dolly Parton song just wouldn't be the same without alternating bass beneath the strumming! It's the perfect opportunity to practice this new technique and recreate the authentic sound of the original.

As usual, scan through the song to get an overview of the structure and a heads up on any potential surprises. This song relies on a steady and reliable rhythmic bass for its feel. Your alternating notes on the lower strings need to be played precisely on the beat.

If it feels like a lot to try at once, why not play just the bass notes picked with the thumb, until you're used to the feel? By the way, if you had a bass guitar, this is exactly the part you would play!

Intro

G

| 4/4 / / / / | / / / / | / / / / | / / / / ‖

Verse

G

| / / / / | / / / / | / / / / | / / / / |

1. Back   through the   years   I   go   wand -'ring once   a - gain,

C

| / / / / | / / / / | / / / / | / / / / |

back   to the   sea - sons of   my   youth.   I   re -

G

| / / / / | / / / / | / / / / | / / / / |

call   a   box   of   rags   that   some - one   gave   us   and

C

| / / / / | / / / / | / / / / | / / / / ‖

how   my   ma - ma   put   the   rags   to   use.   2. There were

Verse

G

‖: / / / / | / / / / | / / / / | / / / / |

(2.) rags   of   man- y   col - ors,   but   ev -'ry piece   was   small,   and I
(3.) sewed   she told   a   sto - ry   from the   Bi - ble   she   had   read,   a - bout a

D

| / / / / | / / / / | / / / / | / / / / |

did - n't   have   a   coat   and it   was   way down   in   the   fall.   Ma - ma
coat   of   man- y   col - ors Jo - seph   wore, and   then   she   said: "Per -

Words and Music by Dolly Parton
Copyright © 1969 (Renewed 1997) Velvet Apple Music
All Rights Reserved   Used by Permission

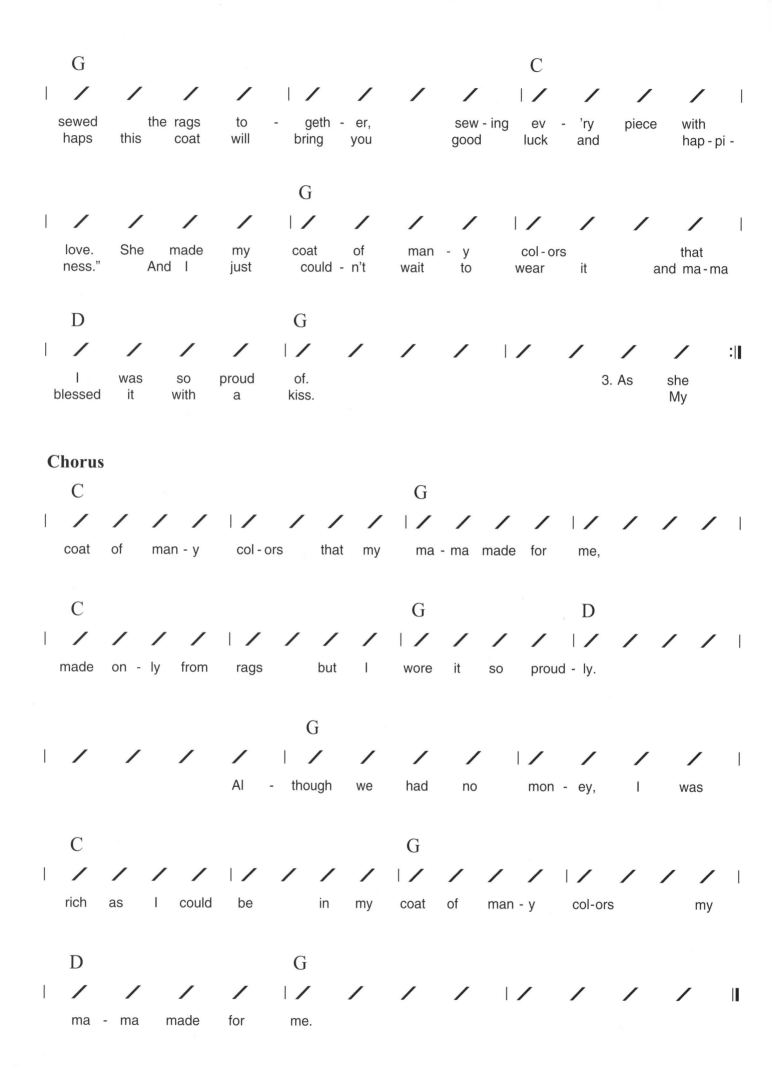

G

sewed   the rags   to - geth - er,

haps this coat will   bring you

C

sew - ing ev - 'ry   piece   with

good   luck and   hap - pi -

G

love. She made   my   coat   of   man - y   col - ors   that

ness." And I   just   could - n't   wait   to   wear   it   and ma - ma

D   **G**

I   was   so   proud   of.   3. As   she

blessed it   with   a   kiss.   My

Chorus

C   **G**

coat   of   man - y   col - ors   that   my   ma - ma made for   me,

C   **G**   **D**

made on - ly from rags   but   I   wore it   so   proud - ly.

G

Al - though we   had   no   mon - ey,   I   was

C   **G**

rich as   I   could be   in   my   coat   of   man - y   col - ors   my

D   **G**

ma - ma made for   me.

THE TIDE IS HIGH

One more song to try with alternating bass, this time a smash hit for Blondie, but originally recorded by the Jamaican group the Paragons back in 1966.

For this song, let's combine the alternating bass with the "boom, chick-a, boom, chick-a" pattern we saw on page 25. For an authentic reggae feel, play the bass notes softly with firm, crisp strums in between.

G

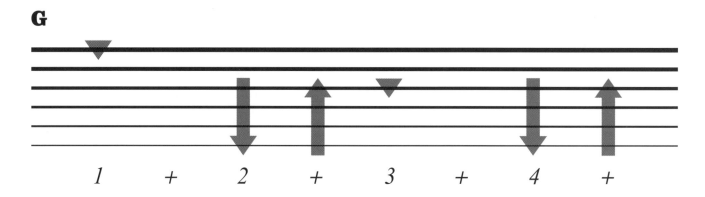

In the song, since the latter half of the chord progression includes two chords (on beats 1 and 3), the strum pattern won't allow for alternating bass on each of those chords. So for each chord in the second bar of the chord progression, you can simply play the main bass note followed by the down-up strum.

One more thing: take a look at the final chorus and you'll see a measure with a horizontal bracket and a number "1" in it, followed by a similar measure numbered "2." These indicate a different ending for the first and second play-through of that chorus. In this example, there's no lyric to sing at the end of the first play-through, but when the chorus comes around again, it ends with the lyric "The…" that takes us into the outro. These two bracketed sections are known as the *first ending* and *second ending*.

Intro

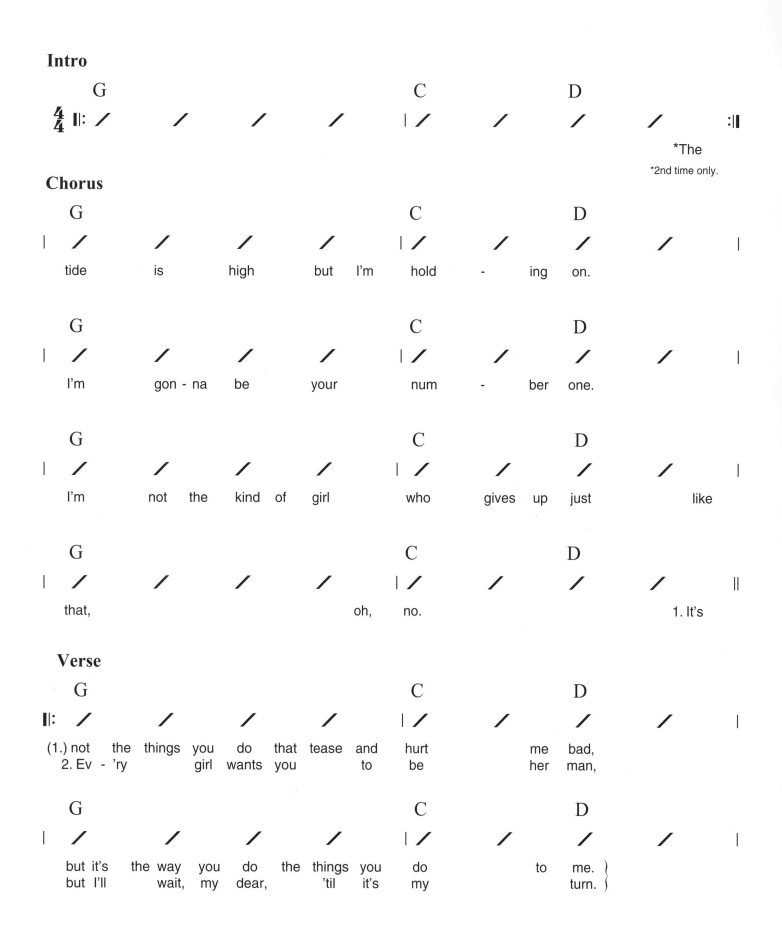

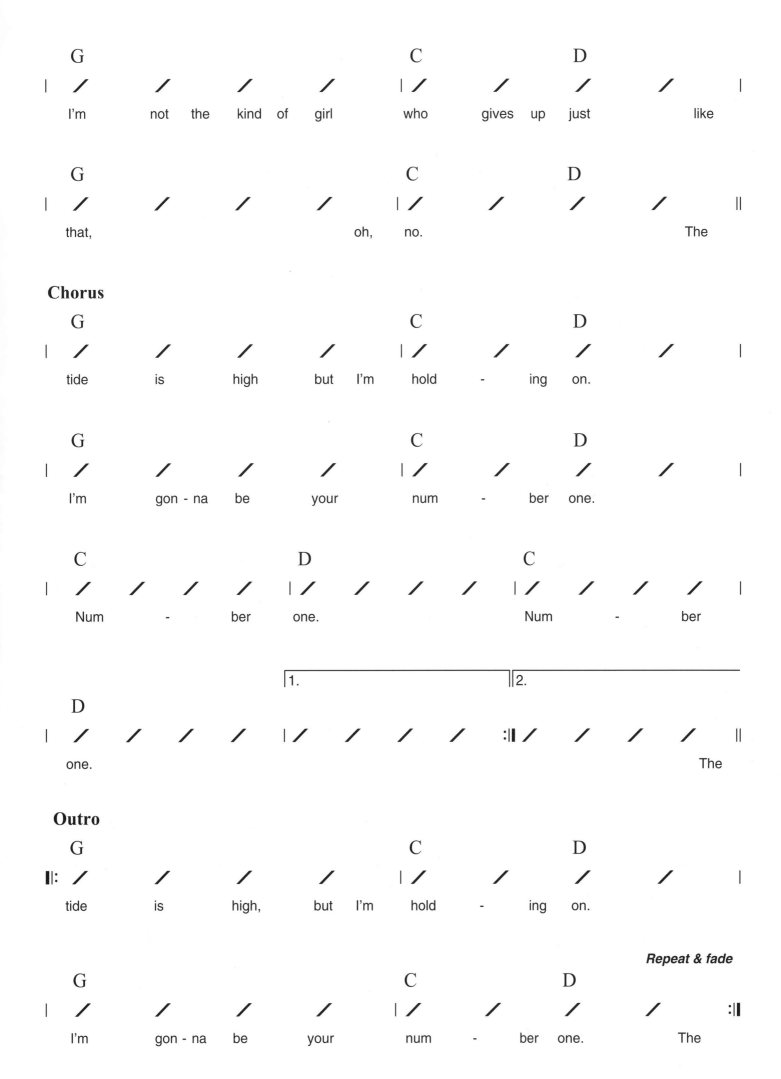

The Tide Is High   35

MORE ON STRUMMING: CREATING NEW PATTERNS

By sticking to a few simple guidelines, you can easily create strumming patterns of your own. Let's take a look at a couple of classic patterns to see what makes them tick.

Looking back at the approach for U2's "I Still Haven't Found What I'm Looking For" (page 22), we played a simple strumming pattern with continuous eighth notes (or "half beats"), strumming down *on* the beat and up *off* the beat.

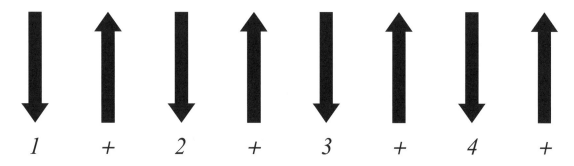

In fact, this basic pattern can be used to create all sorts of variations. For example, try this one in which you'll miss a couple of up-strums.

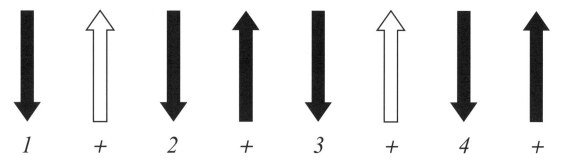

Try counting "down, down-up, down, down-up" to get the feel of this pattern. The crucial thing here is to keep the strumming hand moving down-up-down-up even when you're not making contact with the strings. This will really help with keeping a steady rhythm. As before, the white arrows in the diagram indicate the "silent" hand movement.

Now let's have a bit of fun with this pattern. Instead of playing a down-strum on the third beat, let's delay it until the following "+," which means playing it as an up-strum. Remember to keep your strumming hand moving up and down even when it's not striking the strings. Finally, let's leave out the final up-strum. This pattern doesn't look any trickier than the previous one, but it'll require some concentration. Take it slowly at first, maybe saying "down, down-up, up-down" in time to the strums.

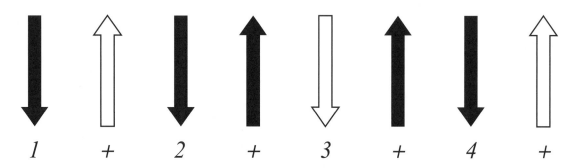

You'll only really get the full flavor of this strumming pattern if you loop it over and over. Try varying the accents on the down-strums and on the up-strums. As already discussed, you'll be surprised how a little tweak can change the feel quite dramatically. Try it on all three chord shapes and play the pattern at different *tempos* (speeds) until it becomes a natural, flowing sequence.

This pattern is one of the most commonly played strumming rhythms of all and once you have it under your fingers, you'll find you come back to it again and again.

USED TO LOVE HER

Next up is a Guns N' Roses number from 1988. Our newest pattern works perfectly for this song. The chords change quite rapidly, so it might be a good idea to start with an earlier pattern. The one we used for "All Apologies" will also work well with this song.

To get used to the pace of changing chords quickly, try playing just the intro section slowly at first. Notice how it repeats, and that the verse is based on exactly the same sequence. Start by strumming a single chord per measure before building up to other patterns.

Intro

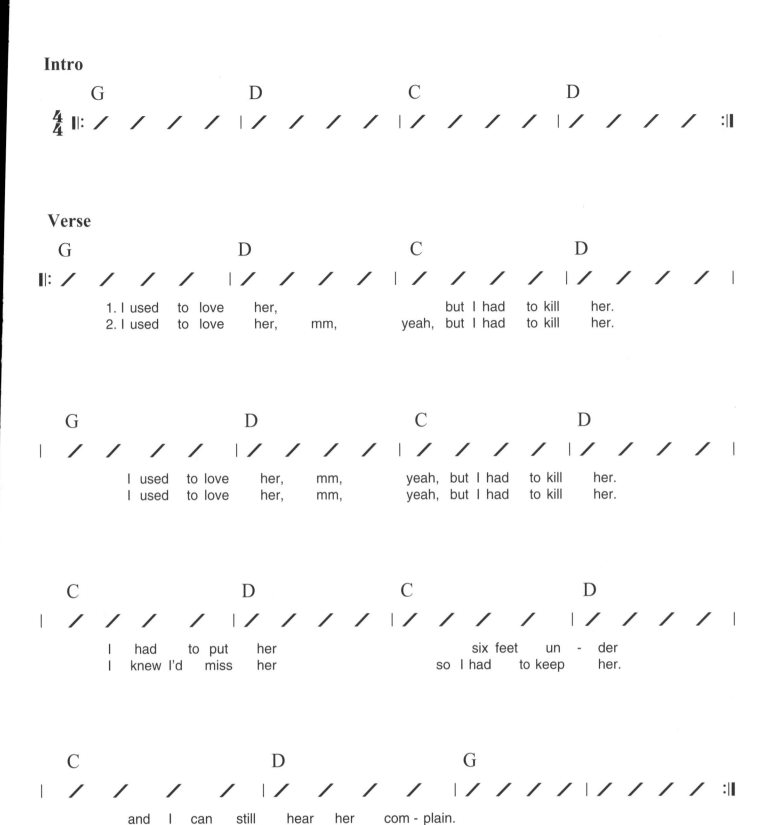

Verse

G D C D

1. I used to love her, but I had to kill her.
2. I used to love her, mm, yeah, but I had to kill her.

G D C D

I used to love her, mm, yeah, but I had to kill her.
I used to love her, mm, yeah, but I had to kill her.

C D C D

I had to put her six feet un - der
I knew I'd miss her so I had to keep her.

C D G

and I can still hear her com - plain.
She's bur - ied right in my back - yard.

Words and Music by W. Axl Rose, Slash, Izzy Stradlin', Duff McKagan and Steven Adler
Copyright © 1988 Guns N' Roses Music (ASCAP) and Black Frog Music (ASCAP)
All Rights for Black Frog Music in the U.S. and Canada Controlled and Administered by Universal - PolyGram International Publishing, Inc.
International Copyright Secured   All Rights Reserved

THREE LITTLE BIRDS

Here's a simple Bob Marley classic that calls for precise, minimal strumming. This time let's play the same pattern we used for "The Tide Is High" (page 33), but without the bass notes.

Having no strums on beats 1 and 3 means you'll have to count very carefully. The down-up strums on beat 2 and again on beat 4 are all you've got, so aim for a very steady and regular feel. As always, keep the strumming hand moving throughout.

If you happen to "catch" the strings when there's supposed to be silence, it doesn't matter too much; it'll sound quite natural and intentional as long as the basic down-up strums on beats 2 and 4 are nice and solid.

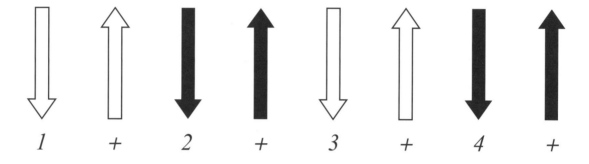

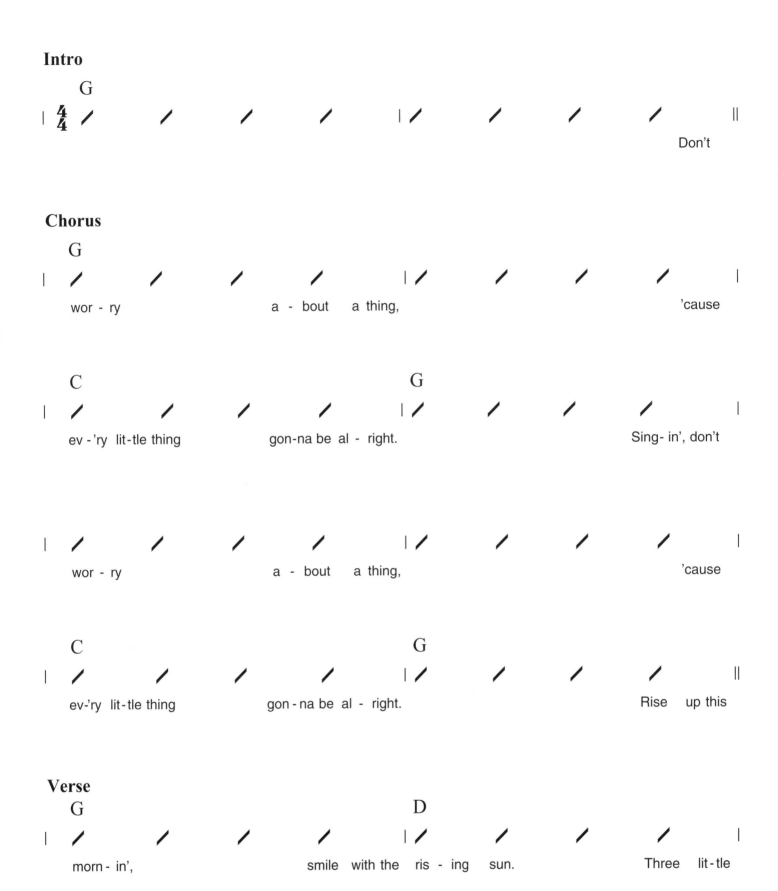

Intro

G

Don't

Chorus

G

wor - ry   a - bout   a thing,   'cause

C   G

ev - 'ry lit-tle thing   gon - na be al - right.   Sing- in', don't

wor - ry   a - bout   a thing,   'cause

C   G

ev - 'ry lit-tle thing   gon - na be al - right.   Rise   up this

Verse

G   D

morn - in',   smile with the ris - ing sun.   Three   lit - tle

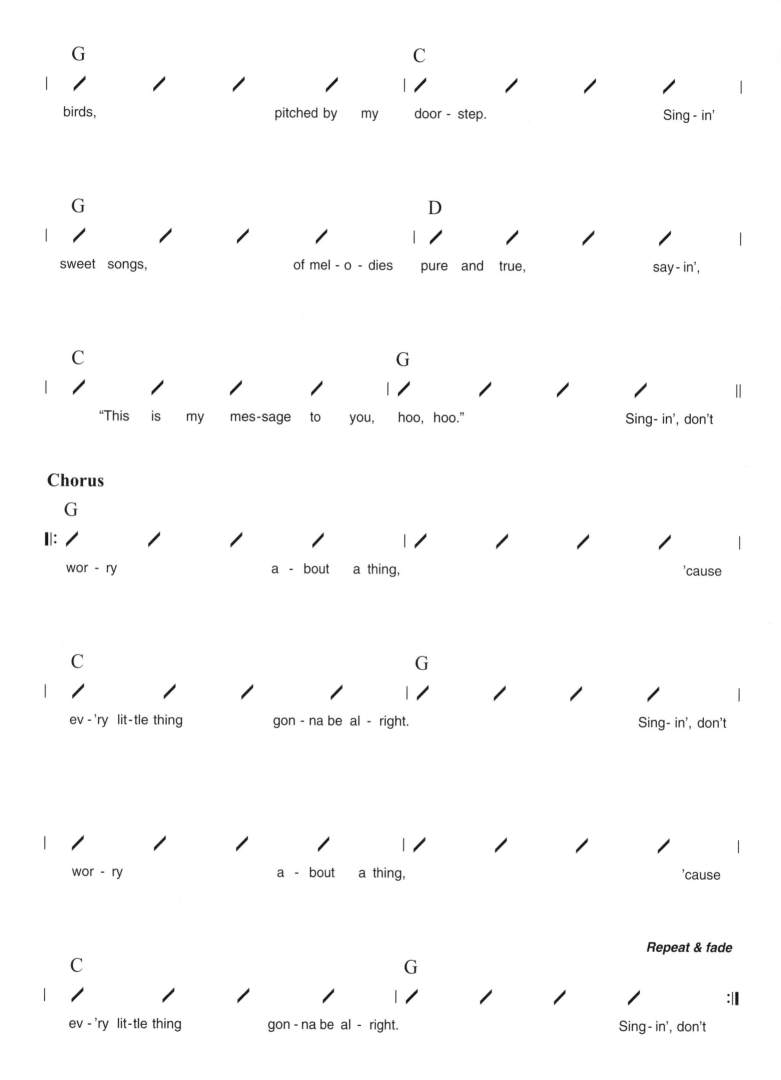

How To Enjoy Guitar With Just Three Chords

THE FIRST CUT IS THE DEEPEST

This song has been a hit for Sheryl Crow and Rod Stewart, but did you know it was actually written by Cat Stevens?

Here's the final pattern from page 36 again. You'll notice the pattern lasts for four beats, while in this song the chords often change every two beats. In practice, this means keeping the pattern going as you change chords—quite a challenge!

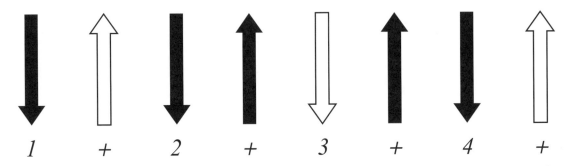

Large sections of the song repeat the same sequence, so try committing them to memory rather than having to read every new chord as it approaches.

By the way, since you're not strumming right on beat 3, if the chord changes here, you won't hear it until the following up-strum. This is fine because it creates some rhythmic interest, and you could try accenting that up-strum to make a feature of it. Alternatively, try moving to the new chord on the up-strum just before beat 3 (this is known as *anticipation*), which will give your playing a more urgent, accented feel. It will take some practice to make this chord change, so try it slowly at first!

Intro

G   C   D

| 4/4 / / / / | / / / / |

G   C   D

| / / / / | / / / / ‖

1. I would have

Verse

G   D   C   D

‖: / / / / | / / / |

(1.) giv - en you all   of my heart,   but there's
(2.) want you by   my side.   Just to

G   D   C   D

| / / / / | / / / |

some - one who's torn it a - part.   And she's
help me dry the tears that I've cried.   And I'm

G   D   C   D

| / / / / | / / / |

tak - en just all   that I had.   But if you want, I'll
sure   gon - na give you a try.   And if you want, I'll

G   D   C   D

| / / / / | / / / |

try to love a - gain.   Ba - by, I'll try
try to love a - gain.   Ba - by, I'll try

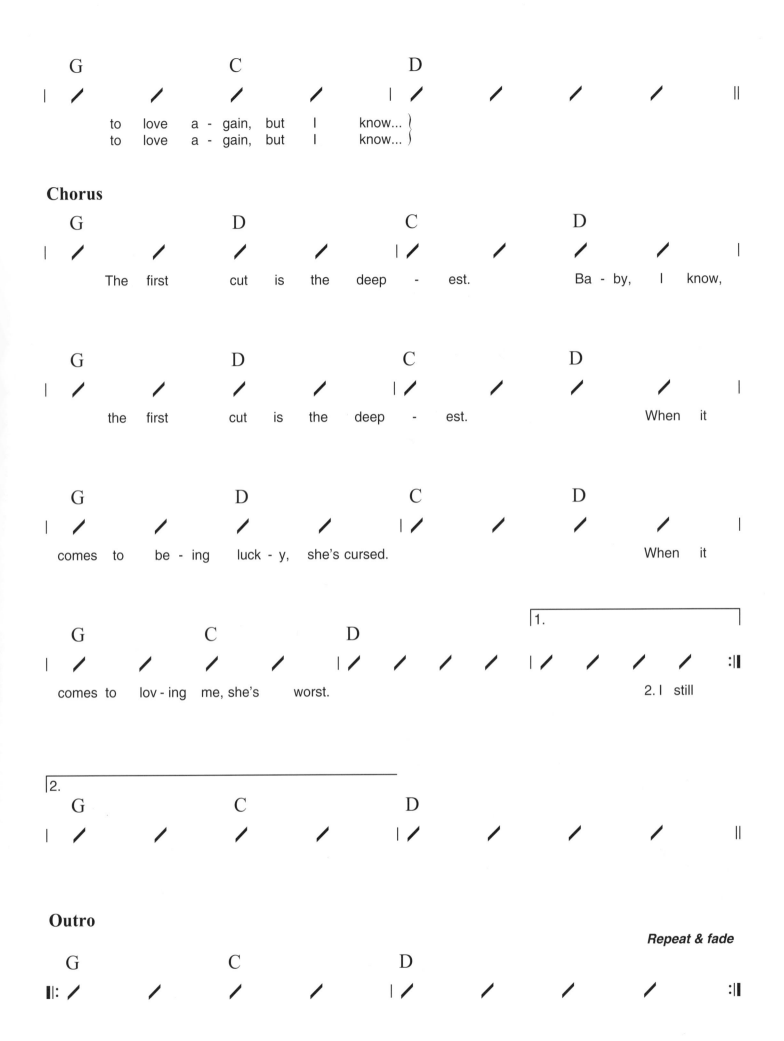

The First Cut Is the Deepest   45

WHAT I GOT

Californian ska-punk band Sublime had a big hit in the '90s that uses just two chords, G and C. In fact, each chord lasts for a bar, so if you can change from G to C within four beats, and back again, you can already play this song! There's plenty of opportunity to focus on accurate and atmospheric strumming since the chords pretty much take care of themselves.

Here's a suggested strumming pattern. There's nothing new here except that you might like to limit the down-strums on beats 1 and 2 to the lower strings. This will help make the song sound more bass-heavy, with the eighth-note strums that follow a little lighter. As always, a solid, even pattern is what drives the music.

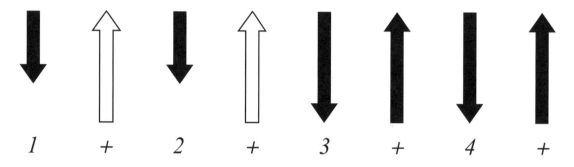

Also notice the lengthy first ending, which is a guitar solo. On the repeat, skip this section and continue straight to the chorus.

Intro

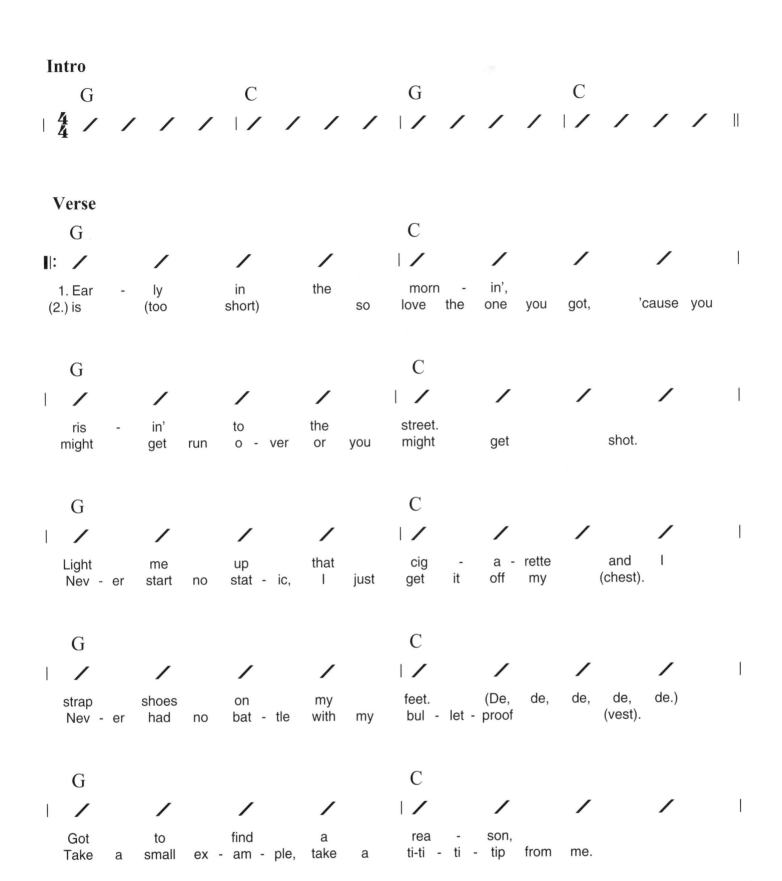

Verse

G   C

‖: /   /   /   / | /   /   /   / |

1. Ear - ly   in   the   morn - in',   so   love the one you got,   'cause you
(2.) is   (too   short)   so   love the one you got,   'cause you

G   C

| /   /   /   / | /   /   /   / |

ris - in'   to   the   street.
might   get   run   o - ver   or   you   might   get   shot.

G   C

| /   /   /   / | /   /   /   / |

Light   me   up   that   cig - a - rette   and   I
Nev - er   start   no   stat - ic,   I   just   get   it   off   my   (chest).

G   C

| /   /   /   / | /   /   /   / |

strap   shoes   on   my   feet. (De, de, de, de, de.)
Nev - er   had   no   bat - tle   with   my   bul - let - proof   (vest).

G   C

| /   /   /   / | /   /   /   / |

Got   to   find   a   rea - son,
Take   a   small   ex - am - ple,   take   a   ti-ti - ti - tip   from   me.

G   /   /   /   /   **C**   /   /   /   /

rea - son things went wrong.
Take all of your mon - ey, give it all (to cha - ri- ty-ty-ty-ty). Love

G   /   /   /   /   **C**   /   /   /   /

Got to find a rea - son why my
is what I got, it's with - in my reach and the

G   /   /   /   /   **C**   /   /   /   /

mon - ey's all gone.
Sub - lime style's still straight from Long Beach. It all

G   /   /   /   /   **C**   /   /   /   /

I got a Dal - ma - tian and
comes back to you, you fin-'lly get what you de - serve.

G   /   /   /   /   **C**   /   /   /   /

I can still get high.
Try to test that, you're bound to get served.

G   /   /   /   /   **C**   /   /   /   /

I can play the gui - tar like a
Love's what I got, don't start a riot. You

G   /   /   /   /   **C**   /   /   /   /

moth - er - fuck - in' riot.
feel it when the dance gets hot.

1.

Guitar Solo

G   C   G   C

| / / / / | / / / / | / / / / | / / / / |

G   C   G   C

| / / / / | / / / / | / / / / | / / / / :||

2. Well, life

2.

Chorus

G   C   G   C

| / / / / | / / / / | / / / / | / / / / |

Lov - in'   is what I   got.   I said re - mem - ber that.

G   C   G   C

| / / / / | / / / / | / / / / | / / / / |

Lov - in'   is what I   got,   and re - mem - ber that.

G   C   G   C

| / / / / | / / / / | / / / / | / / / / |

Lov - in'   is what I   got.   I said re - mem - ber that.

G   C   G

| / / / / | / / / / | / / / / | / / / / ||

Lov - in'   is what I   got,   I   got, I   got, I   got.

Chuck Berry's 1964 rock 'n' roll hit has a subtly different rhythmic feel than the other songs we've looked at so far.

Instead of the beats being split into two, they're now divided into groups of three—known as *triplets*. These triplets are counted "*one*-and-a-*two*-and-a-*three*-and-a-*four*-and-a." As before, you'll want your strumming hand to move constantly down and up. Here's how the strums coincide with the beats.

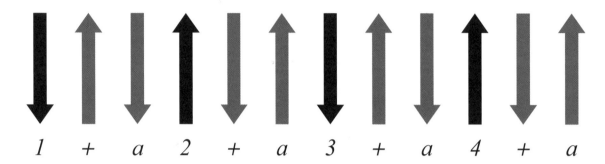

1 + a 2 + a 3 + a 4 + a

For the intro, try playing every single strum in the pattern for the first measure, twelve in all, stopping with one down-strum on the first beat of the following bar. Pay attention to the "N.C." (no chord) marking above the second beat of every other measure and listen to the original to see just how this works—the verses fly by pretty quickly! This same rhythmic idea continues throughout the verse as well.

By the way, notice the first D chord has a "+" next to it. In this instance, the plus sign has nothing to do with counting. Instead, when attached to a chord, it is a musical symbol meaning "augmented." At this point, you don't need to know anything more about it than this: the standard D chord shape is modified by placing a finger on the 3rd string one fret higher than usual, as shown in the diagram. In fact, you'll probably want to use your first finger on the top string and then re-finger the shape accordingly. This variant of plain D will give you the sound of the original.

The other D chords in the song are played using the standard shape.

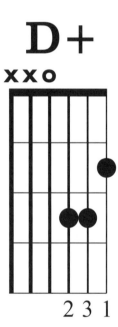

D+

Intro

D+

| 4/4 / / / / | / / / / ‖

N.C.

1. Rid-ing a-long in my au-to-mo-

Verse

G

‖: / / / / | / / / / |

N.C.

(1.) bile, my ba-by be-side me at the
(2.) bile, I was anx-ious to tell her the way I
(3.) go, so we parked way out on the Ko - ko-
(4.) boose, still try-ing to get her belt a

G

| / / / / | / / / / |

N.C.

wheel. I stole a kiss at the turn of a
feel. So I told her soft - ly and sin -
mo. The night was young and the moon was
loose. All the way home I held a

C

| / / / / | / / / / |

N.C.

mile, my cu - ri - os - i - ty run - ning
cere, and she leaned and whis - pered in my
gold, so we both de - cid - ed to take a
grudge, for the safe - ty belt that would - n't

G

| / / / / | / / / / |

N.C.

wild. Cruis - ing and play-ing the ra - di -
ear. Cud - dlin' more and driv - ing
stroll. Can you i - ma-gine the way I
budge. Cruis-ing and play-ing the ra - di -

D

| / / / / | / / / / |

N.C.

o, with no par - tic - u - lar place to
slow, with no par - tic - u - lar place to
felt? I could-n't un-fas-ten her safe - ty
o, with no par - tic - u - lar place to

G

| / / / / | / / / :‖

N.C.

Play 4 times

go. Rid-ing a-long in my au-to-mo-
go. No par - tic - u - lar place to
belt. Rid-ing a-long in my ca - la-
go.

SWEET HOME ALABAMA

Lynyrd Skynyrd's Southern anthem is simple and very repetitive. If you just learn the first two bars of the intro, you'll breeze through the whole song!

Let's try another pick-strum variation by playing a pair of eighth notes in the bass before a single strum on the following beat. Here's how this would look for the first measure.

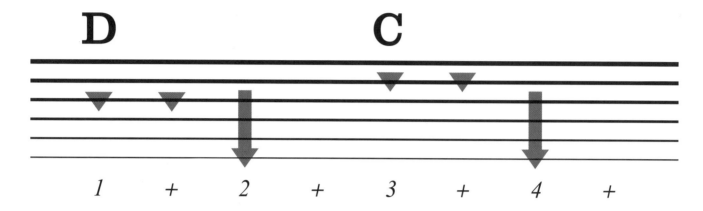

Another space-saving repeat symbol is used in this song. You'll notice the curly, stylized "S" at the start of the verse—this is known as the "sign," usually referred to by the Italian word *segno*. It's often used to mark a point in the song to return to when repeats aren't appropriate (in this song, we're already using repeats and endings for the verse and chorus). Take a look at the end of the song and you'll see "D.S. (take 2nd ending)." "D.S." means *dal segno* (from the sign), so all it really means is go back to the sign and play to the end from there, jumping to the 2nd ending as indicated. Easy!

1.

Interlude

D		C		G			
/	/	/	/	/	/	/	/

D		C		G			
/	/	/	/	/	/	/	/	:‖

2.

Chorus

D		C		G			
/	/	/	/	/	/	/	/

Sweet　　home　　Al - a - bam - a,

D		C		G			
/	/	/	/	/	/	/	/

where　the　skies　　are　so　blue.

D		C		G			
/	/	/	/	/	/	/	/

Sweet　　home　　Al - a - bam - a,

D		C		G			
/	/	/	/	/	/	/	/	‖

Lord,　I'm　com - in'　home　to　you.

Interlude

D		C		G			
/	/	/	/	/	/	/	/

D.S.
(take 2nd ending)

D		C		G			
/	/	/	/	/	/	/	/	‖

THE JOKER

Although this Steve Miller Band song seems to have a similar feel to "Sweet Home Alabama," the basic beat count is at half the speed with the beats divided into four, creating sixteenth notes.

Listen to the acoustic guitar strumming on the original and you'll hear a light, rapid texture that feels very full, even at the slow tempo. *Sixteenth notes* are traditionally counted as "*one*-e-and-a-*two*-e-and-a-*three*-e-and-a-*four*-e-and-a." Here's what constant sixteenths look like in our familiar strumming diagram format.

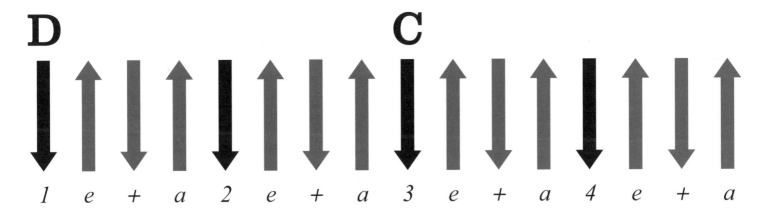

Let's refine this a bit with some bass-heavy strums at the start of each new chord followed by flowing sixteenths. Don't forget to keep the strumming hand moving throughout. It might look something like this.

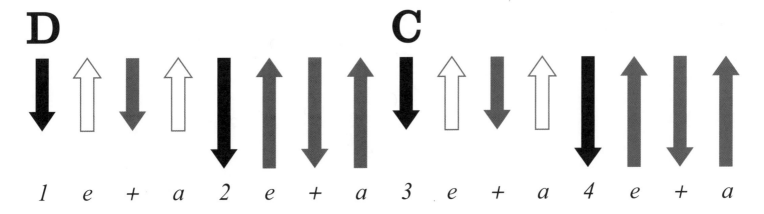

Verse

G   C   D   C

| 4/4 /   /   /   / | /   /   /   / |

1. Some peo - ple call me the space cow - boy.   Yeah,

G   C   D   C

| /   /   /   / | /   /   /   / |

some call me the gang-ster of love.

G   C   D   C

| /   /   /   / | /   /   /   / |

Some peo - ple call me Mau - rice,   'cause I

G   C   D   C

| /   /   /   / | /   /   /   / ||

speak of the pomp-a-tus of love.

𝄋 Verse

G   C   D   C

||: /   /   /   / | /   /   /   / |

2. Peo - ple talk a - bout me, ba - by.

3. You're the cut - est thing that I ev - er did see. |

G   C   D   C

| /   /   /   / | /   /   /   / |

Say I'm do - ing you wrong, do - ing you wrong.

real - ly love your peach - es, want to shake your tree.

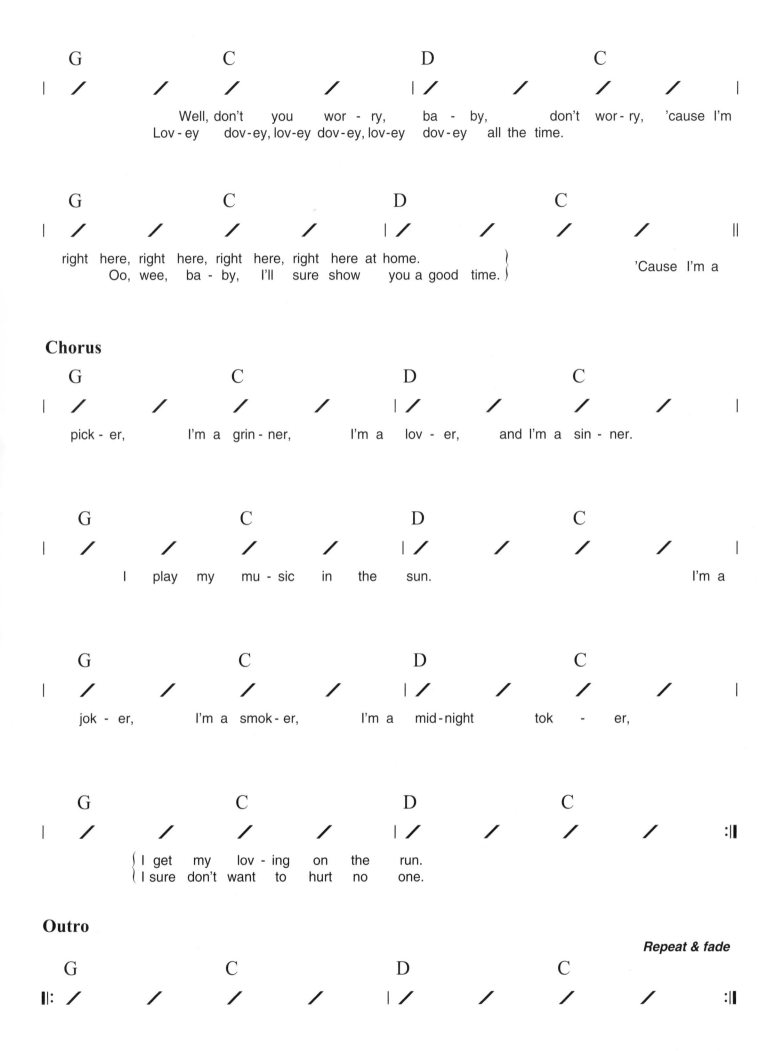

Chorus

Outro

LOVE ME DO

The Beatles' repertoire of chord shapes grew alongside their songwriting skills. However, their first single release "Love Me Do" uses only our three chords… and requires only two of them for the bulk of the song!

Let's return to a pattern we first looked at on the bottom of page 36. It's perfect for this song; listen to the original and hear how the strummed guitar pattern coincides with the tambourine, playing the accents on beats 2 and 4 (the backbeats). Now try accenting these beats in your strumming too.

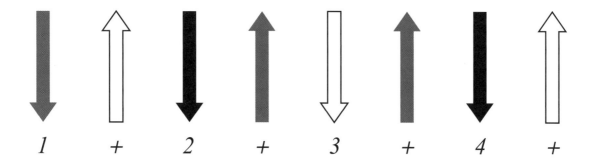

The music uses a variation of the segno that we saw in "Sweet Home Alabama." This time, after the final chorus, we have "D.S. al Coda." A *coda* is a section added to the end of a piece of music (coda is Italian for "tail"). When we reach this instruction, we go back to the sign and play the bridge again, until we come across the instruction "To Coda" (along with a special coda symbol) within the chorus. Now we skip to the coda (the final line).

Intro

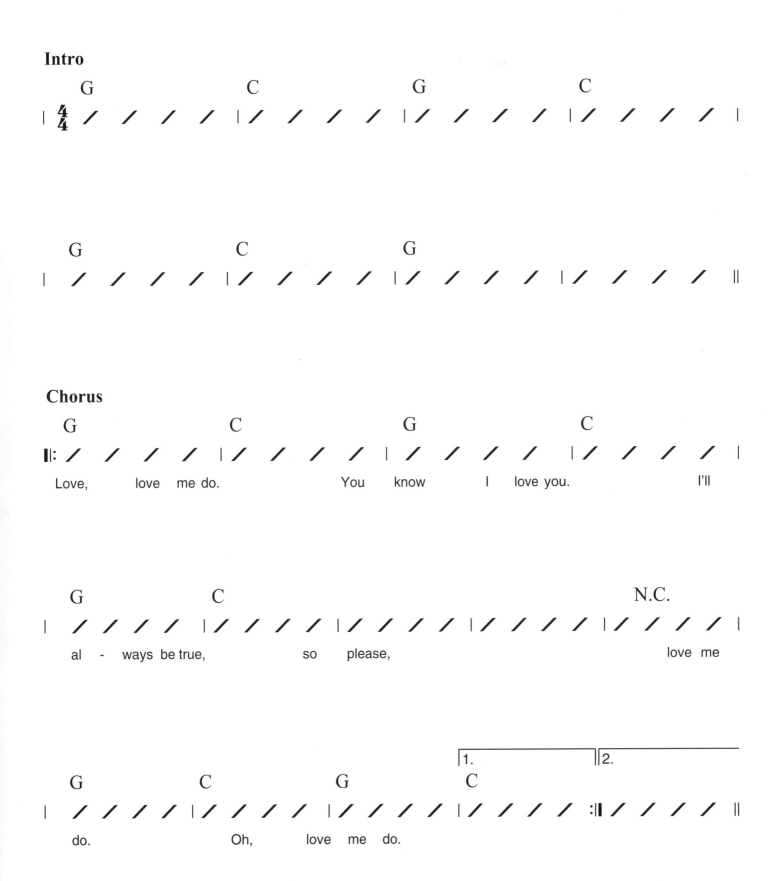

Chorus

G   C   G   C

Love,   love me do.   You   know   I   love you.   I'll

G   C   N.C.

al - ways be true,   so   please,   love me

1.   2.

G   C   G   C

do.   Oh,   love me do.

𝄋 Bridge

D   **C**   **G**

| / / / / | / / / / | / / / / | / / / / |

1. Some - one to love,   some - bod - y new,
2. *Instrumental*

D   **C**   **G**   **N.C.**

| / / / / | / / / / | / / / / | / / / / ‖

some - one to love,   some - one like you.

Chorus

G   **C**   **G**   **C**

| / / / / | / / / / | / / / / | / / / / |

Love,   love me do.   You know   I love you.   I'll

G   **C**   **N.C.**

| / / / / | / / / / | / / / / | / / / / |

al - ways be true,   so please,   love me

To Coda ⊕   *D.S. al Coda*

G   **C**   **G**

| / / / / | / / / / | / / / / | / / / / ‖

do.   Oh,   love me do.   Yeah.

⊕ Coda

Repeat & fade

G   **C**

‖: / / / / | / / / / :‖

love me do.   Oh,

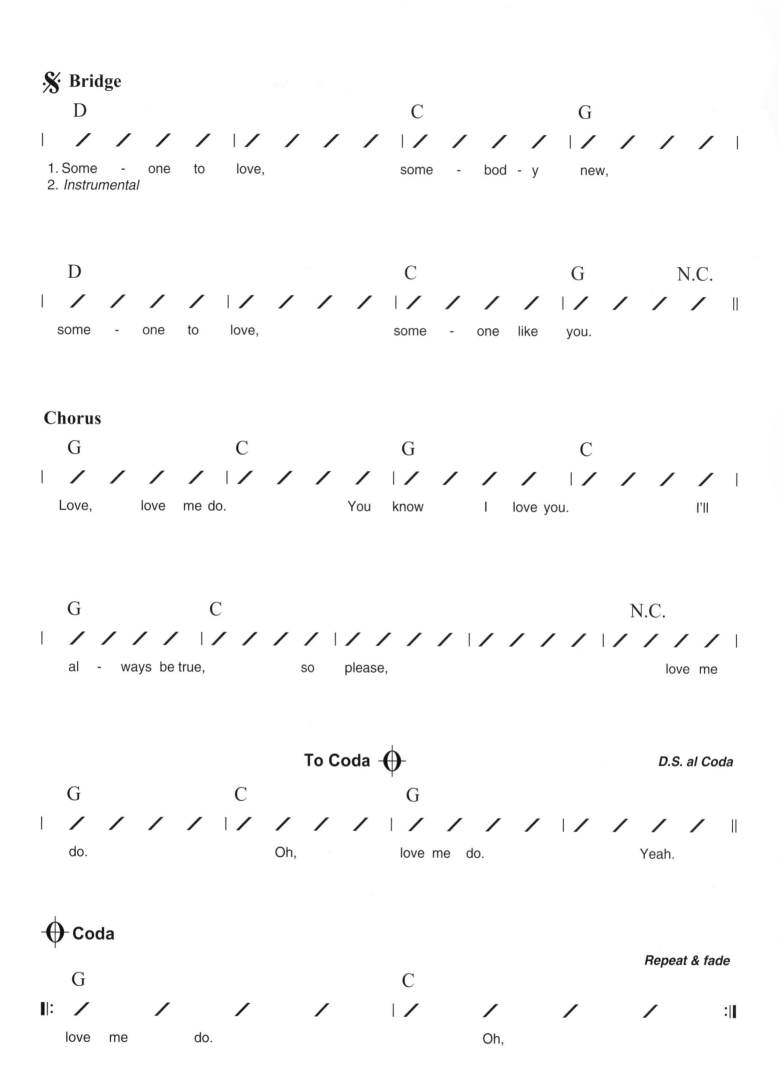

CHASING CARS

Snow Patrol's 2006 single entered the charts in the U.S. after being featured on the popular television show *Grey's Anatomy*.

This song builds almost continuously in terms of volume and energy. Try playing a single, full strum at the start of each measure throughout the verses—that's two measures for each chord—letting the chord ring as long as you can before moving onto the new shape.

Then, as the energy builds in the chorus, transition into an eighth-note strumming pattern like this one, with shorter strums on beats 1 and 3, and fuller, more expansive strums on beats 2 and 4. You'll find that tweaking the accents and precise contrast between the different strums will give you a wide range of expression.

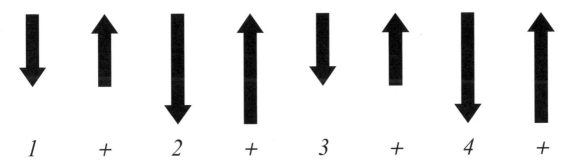

Here's a variation on the standard C chord shape, now with a note added on the 3rd fret of the 2nd string, which you'll fret with your fourth finger. This is optional, as the familiar C shape will work fine, but this version—called Cadd9—will make your performance sound even closer to the original!

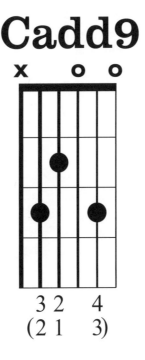

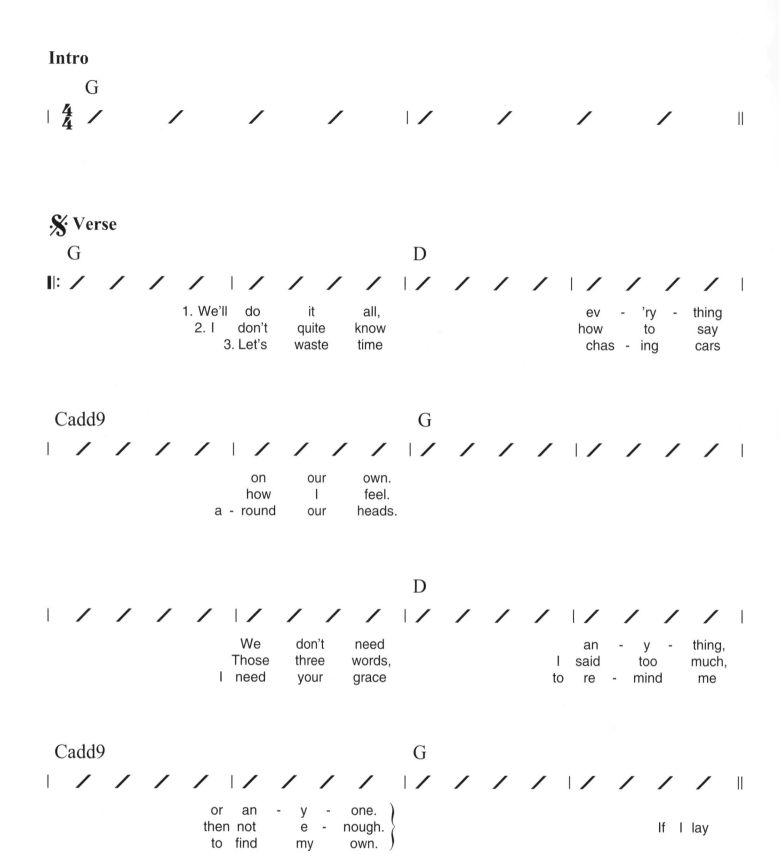

Chorus

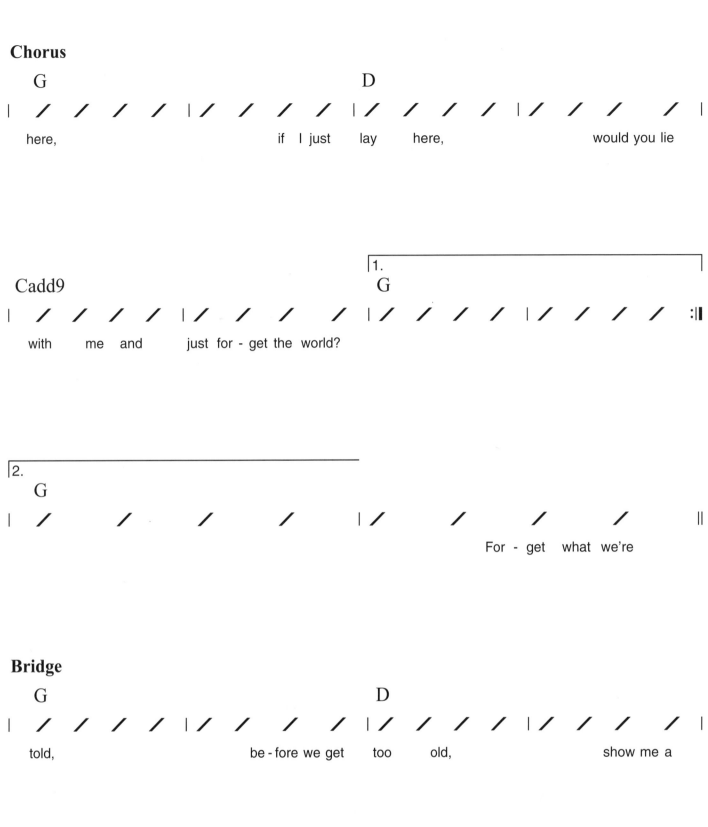

G   **D**

here,   if I just lay here,   would you lie

Cadd9   *1.*   **G**

with me and just for - get the world?

2.   **G**

For - get what we're

Bridge

G   **D**

told,   be - fore we get too old,   show me a

D.S.
(take 2nd ending)

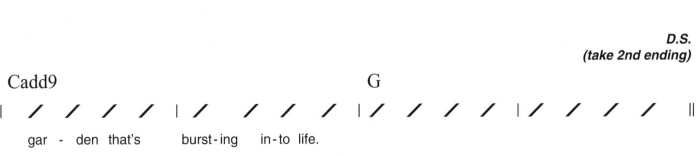

Cadd9   **G**

gar - den that's burst - ing in - to life.

FINGERPICKING

Apart from strumming, another important right-hand technique is fingerpicking. As with strumming, fingerpicking involves playing a repeating pattern. A few simple picking patterns are all you'll need to create effective accompaniments.

FINGERPICKING BASICS

You've already made a start with fingerpicking by playing single thumb notes in pick-strum patterns. Now it's time to look at the rest of the right-hand fingers. Typically, you'll use the first, second, and third fingers on the top three strings.

The thumb is free to play any of the lower strings, providing bass notes that give rhythmic and tonal structure to the patterns we play.

Try to keep the front of the guitar facing out rather than tipping it up to see what you're doing. This way, you'll maintain a more relaxed hand position for smooth and comfortable strumming.

Practice plucking each of the top three strings with the appropriate finger and try to make sure the finger returns to a "ready" position after it has plucked the string. With proper technique, you'll be able to create smooth, repeating patterns.

A SIMPLE PICKING PATTERN

Now let's take a look at a really simple pattern that uses the thumb and all three fingers. For now, play each new string on the beat, counting "one-two-three-four" before repeating. Aim for a steady beat and a nice even volume. Here's how it looks on a C chord.

C

Thumb (T)	Index (1)	Middle (2)	Ring (3)

1 + 2 + 3 + 4 +

The thumb picks the 5th string on beat 1, followed by the first, second, and third fingers in order. Try the same thing on the D and G chords too. For D, the thumb will pick the 4th string; for G, the thumb will pick the 6th string.

VARIATIONS

Now let's take it up a gear. Here's the same pattern, but this time using eighth notes, creating two patterns per measure.

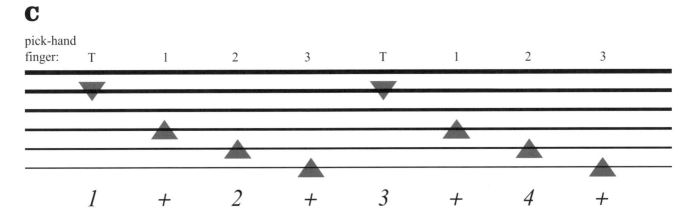

As you play, try to pick the strings evenly. Listen to the way the note on the top string rings out as the pattern restarts on beat 3. Eventually, the goal is to create a sequence of movements that naturally unfolds without having to think about each individual note. You'll soon find that it starts to become smoother. Try it at different speeds until it feels more natural.

You'll be amazed at how versatile this pattern is! Try tweaking the accents a little, maybe emphasizing the 2nd string, and you'll find the pattern starts to sound very different. Continue to practice at different speeds and you'll improve your control.

Since this pattern is now actually two identical patterns in a single measure, there are all sorts of options for adding a bit of variety. One really popular way to create some interest is to introduce an alternating bass, just like we saw on page 28. Here's an example, again on the C chord:

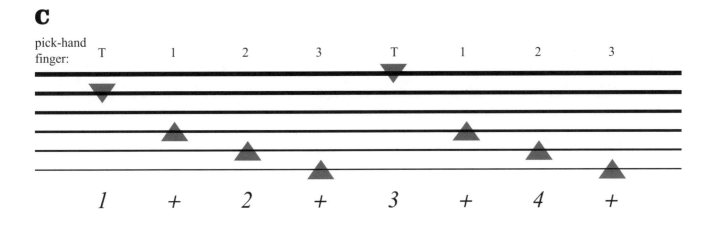

And while we're at it, let's create a variation in the fingers. This time the first half of the pattern remains the same, while in the second part the final note is played on the 3rd string. This means that we only hear the top string once, right before beat 3. If you let it ring out over the remainder of the pattern, it will create a really interesting feel.

C

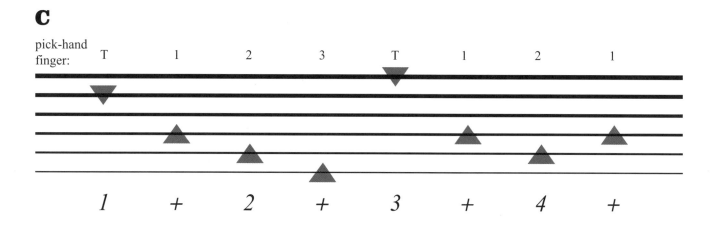

Try the same thing using the other shapes, but with the bass notes adjusted to suit the chord.

G

D

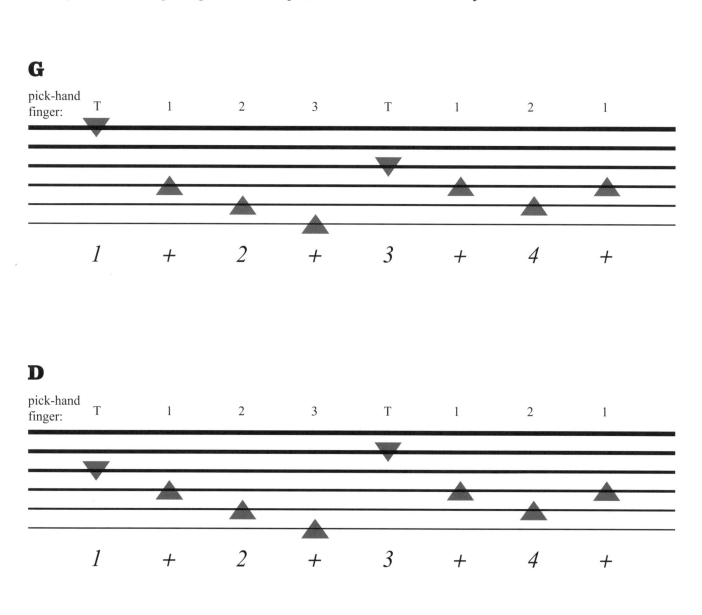

MORE VARIATIONS

Of course, you can play any combination of strings you like in any order. The only limits are your imagination… and your technique! However, you'll probably want to keep a bass note at the start of the pattern. This helps to establish the chord at the beginning of each measure while promoting a solid rhythm moving forward. Beyond that, you could try different combinations of fingers, maybe even playing two strings together. Here are a few suggestions, all on a C chord (though you can naturally adapt these for D and G too).

In the first pattern, the bass note on beat 1 is followed by a sequence of fingerpicked notes like a ripple. Try to make sure the bass note sounds beneath the entire measure and that the note on the top string is allowed to ring out too.

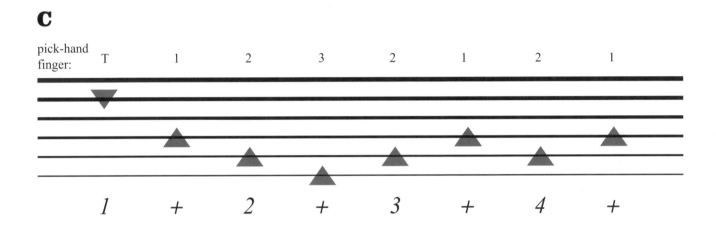

Now for a pattern that works really well at a slow tempo. Here it is shown with alternating bass, but that's not obligatory. The second and third fingers pick together on beats 2 and 4.

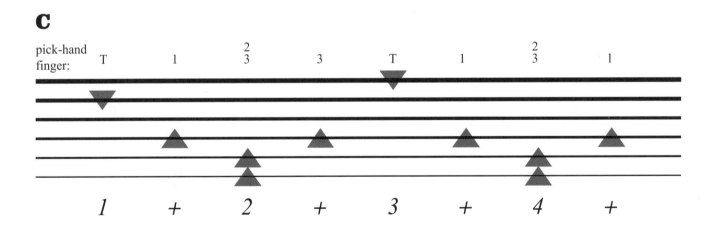

Finally, let's look at a pattern with the fingers out of sequence—that is, with a jump from the top string to the third string after each bass note. This versatile pattern can be very expressive, especially if you vary the accents to emphasize different strings at certain points.

C

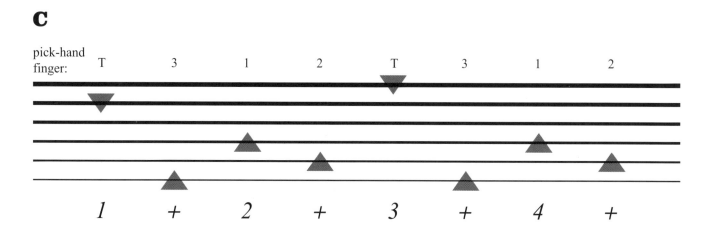

LEAVING ON A JET PLANE

John Denver's classic is perfect for some fingerpicking. You might want to get used to the sequence first by playing it through with a pick-strum pattern like the ones we saw on page 25.

Once you're familiar with the overall feel and structure of the song, try a simple quarter-note pattern like this. We've been using quarter-note values in many of our patterns up until this point; a quarter note requires only a single strum or pick to fill up one whole beat.

G

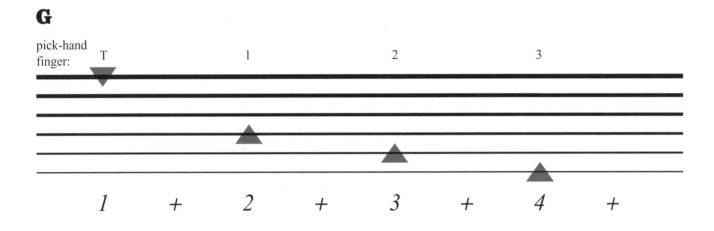

The next example is a flowing eighth-note pattern that's ideal for this song once you're feeling confident. It'll require careful counting and a nice, relaxed technique, but it's worth the effort. Naturally, you'll want to change the bass string for each different chord.

G

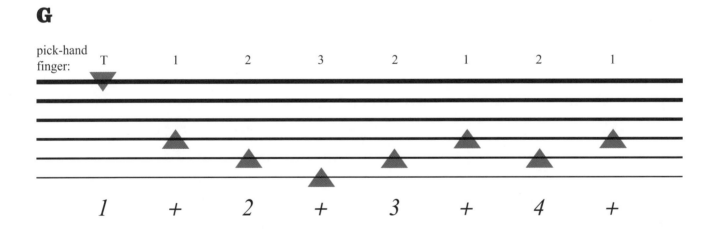

Intro

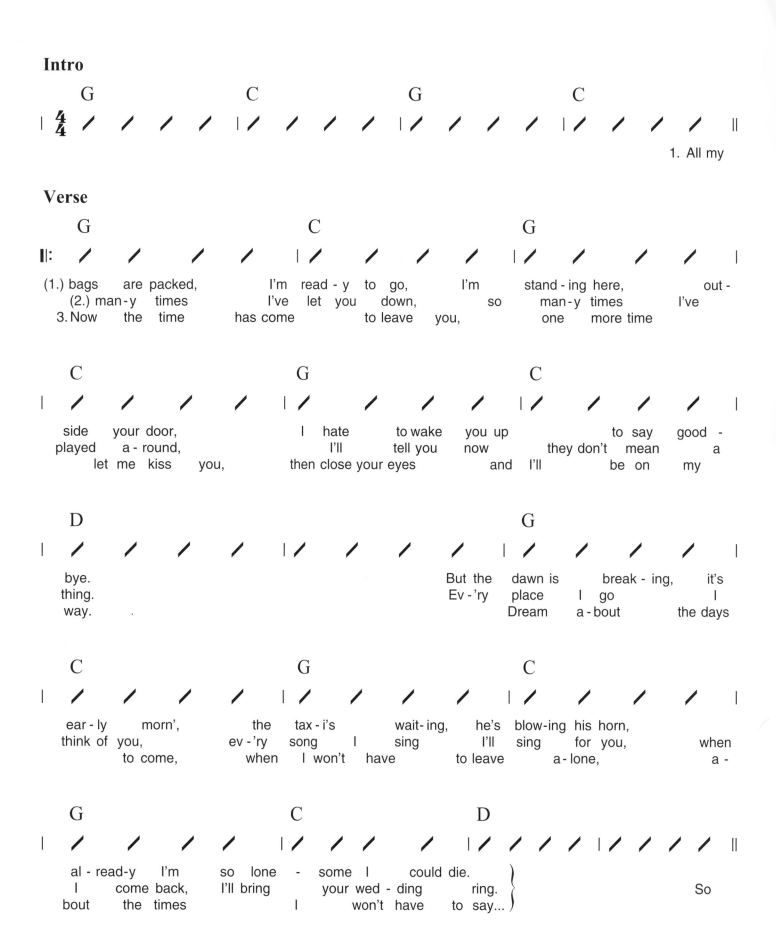

G   C   G   C

| 4/4 ╱ ╱ ╱ ╱ | ╱ ╱ ╱ ╱ | ╱ ╱ ╱ ╱ | ╱ ╱ ╱ ╱ ‖

1. All my

Verse

G   C   G

‖: ╱ ╱ ╱ ╱ | ╱ ╱ ╱ ╱ | ╱ ╱ ╱ ╱ |

(1.) bags   are packed,   I'm read - y to go,   I'm   stand - ing here,   out -
(2.) man-y times   I've let you down,   so   man-y times   I've
3. Now the time   has come   to leave you,   one   more time

C   G   C

| ╱ ╱ ╱ ╱ | ╱ ╱ ╱ ╱ | ╱ ╱ ╱ ╱ |

side   your door,   I hate   to wake you up   to say good -
played a - round,   I'll   tell you now   they don't mean   a
let me kiss   you,   then close your eyes   and I'll   be on   my

D   G

| ╱ ╱ ╱ ╱ | ╱ ╱ ╱ ╱ | ╱ ╱ ╱ ╱ |

bye.   But the dawn is   break - ing, it's
thing.   Ev - 'ry place I go   I
way.   .   Dream a - bout   the days

C   G   C

| ╱ ╱ ╱ ╱ | ╱ ╱ ╱ ╱ | ╱ ╱ ╱ ╱ |

ear - ly   morn',   the tax - i's   wait - ing, he's blow-ing his horn,
think of you,   ev - 'ry song I   sing   I'll sing   for you,   when
to come,   when I won't have   to leave a - lone,   a -

G   C   D

| ╱ ╱ ╱ ╱ | ╱ ╱ ╱ ╱ | ╱ ╱ ╱ ╱ | ╱ ╱ ╱ ╱ ‖

al - read-y I'm   so lone - some I   could die.   ⎫
I   come back, I'll bring   your wed - ding   ring. ⎬   So
bout the times   I   won't have to say... ⎭

Pre-Chorus

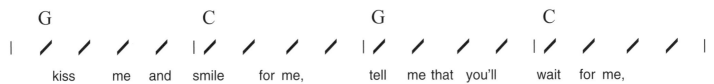

G   C   G   C

kiss   me   and   smile   for me,   tell   me that you'll   wait   for me,

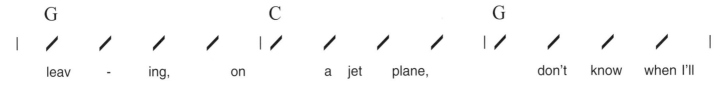

G   C   D

hold me like you'll   nev-er   let me go.   'Cause, I'm

Chorus

G   C   G

leav   -   ing,   on   a   jet   plane,   don't   know   when I'll

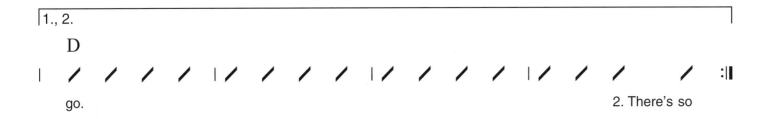

C   G   C

be back   a-gain.   Oh,   babe,   I   hate   to

1., 2.

D

go.   2. There's so

3.

D   G

go.

WHEN YOU SAY NOTHING AT ALL

Originally a hit for country star Keith Whitley back in Christmas 1988, then for Alison Krauss in '95, it's best known in the UK as the first solo single by Ronan Keating, where it topped the charts in 1999.

This song is ideal for a simple fingerpicking accompaniment. In the intro and verse, the chords mostly change every two beats, so a straightforward eighth-note pattern is called for. Something like the pattern below would be perfect.

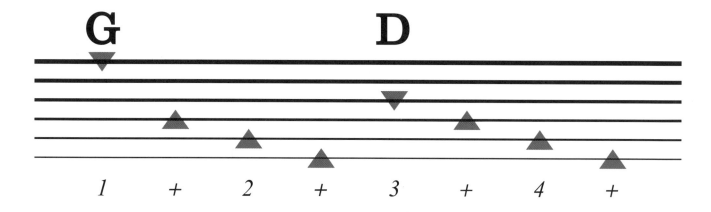

As the music builds in volume in the chorus, you might like to switch to a strumming pattern instead. Combining strumming and fingerpicking in different sections is a great way to create a varied and interesting accompaniment. Here's our old faithful strumming pattern—it's just right for the chorus.

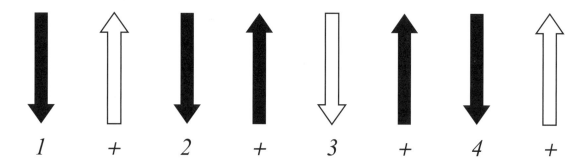

One more thing: take a look at the measure right before the chorus. It only has two beats! You'll need to count carefully so as not to lose your place. It's literally just half the length of the other measures.

Intro

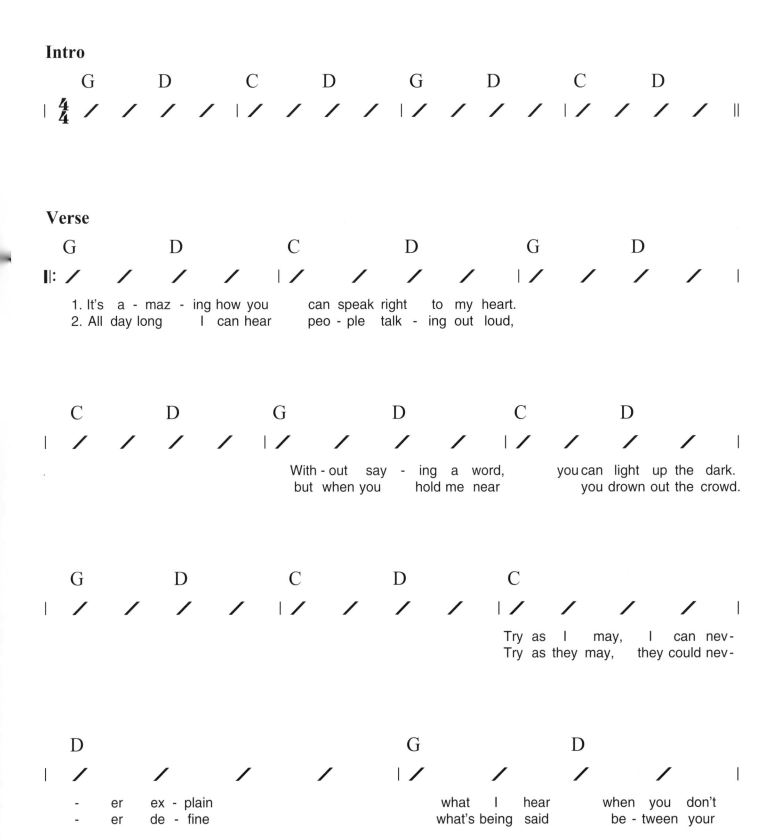

| G | D | C | D | G | D | C | D |

| 4/4 / / / / | / / / / | / / / / | / / / / ||

Verse

| G | D | C | D | G | D |

||: / / / / | / / / / | / / / / |

1. It's a - maz - ing how you   can speak right   to my heart.
2. All day long   I can hear   peo - ple talk - ing out loud,

| C | D | G | D | C | D |

| / / / / | / / / / | / / / / |

With - out say - ing a word,   you can light up the dark.
but when you   hold me near   you drown out the crowd.

| G | D | C | D | C |

| / / / / | / / / / | / / / / |

Try as I may,   I can nev -
Try as they may,   they could nev -

| D | G | D |

| / / / / | / / / / |

- er ex - plain   what I hear   when you don't
- er de - fine   what's being said   be - tween your

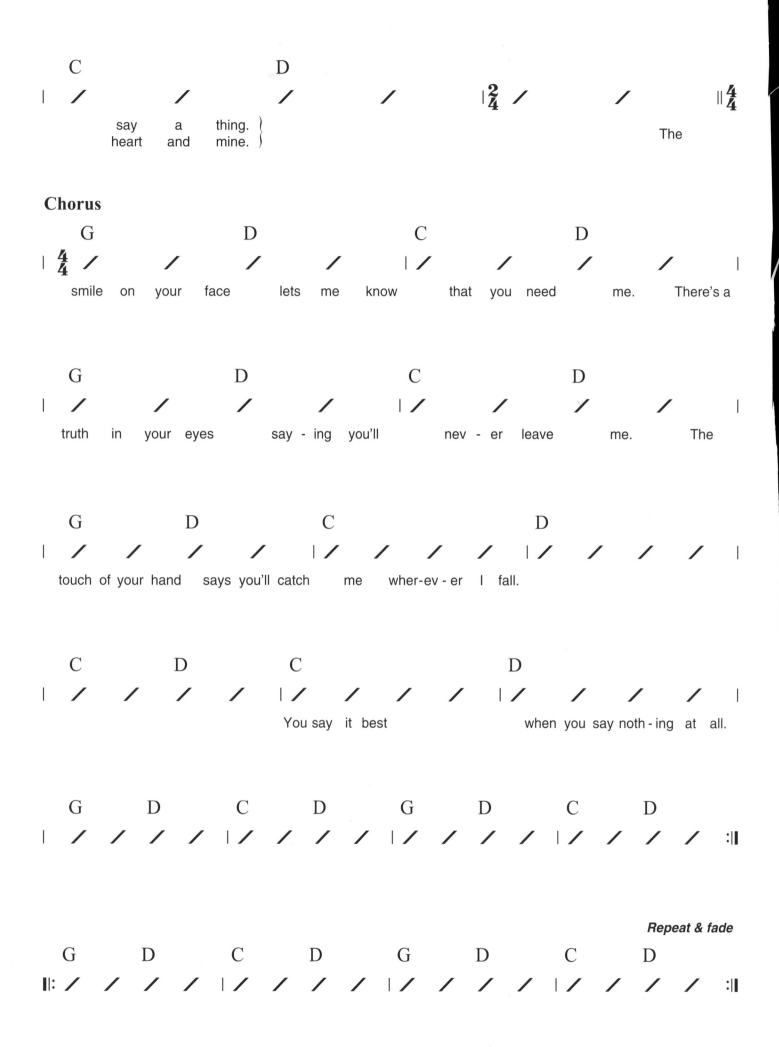

C   /   /   D   /   /   **2/4** /   /   **4/4**

say   a   thing.)
heart   and   mine.)
                          The

Chorus

G   D   C   D

smile on your face   lets me know   that you need   me.   There's a

G   D   C   D

truth in your eyes   say - ing you'll   nev - er leave   me.   The

G   D   C   D

touch of your hand   says you'll catch   me   wher-ev - er   I   fall.

C   D   C   D

You say it best   when you say noth - ing at all.

G   D   C   D   G   D   C   D

Repeat & fade

G   D   C   D   G   D   C   D

USING A CAPO

A capo opens up all sorts of opportunities for your guitar playing, allowing you to play in virtually any key with just a few simple chords.

All the songs in this book can be played with a maximum of three chord shapes. As long as you're playing the right chord at the right time, it'll sound fine. For example, if you play along with the original recording of "Love Me Do" you'll find you're playing at the same *pitch* as the Beatles. The pitch is the proper term for how high or low a piece of music sounds.

However, try playing along to the original recording of "Coat of Many Colors" and you'll hear that your guitar part sounds a bit too low. That's because Dolly Parton's version is in a different *key*. Basically, that means that all of the notes in her version sound like they are the equivalent of three frets higher when using these chord shapes.

There's an easy fix: an inexpensive but indispensable little gizmo that no guitarist should be without, known as a *capo*. Capos come in various forms, but they all do the same thing. When placed around the fingerboard over the strings, they effectively raise the pitch of the guitar by a given number of frets.

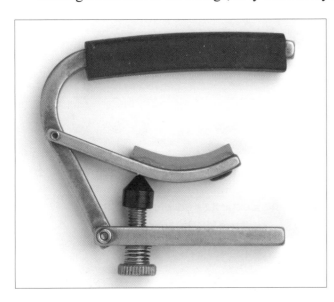 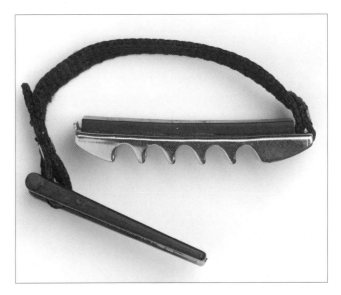

Make sure the capo fits snugly—but not too tightly—around the neck, with the fretting bar lying flat across the fingerboard and not bending the strings away from their natural straight course. You might need to experiment a little, moving the capo closer to or farther from the metal fretwire for the best sound. Depending on the type of capo you have, the orientation of the capo may also affect the comfort of your fretting hand.

For "Coat of Many Colors," place the capo over the strings at the 3rd fret. Try to make sure that you're not tightening the capo too much and that the strings aren't bent, which could make them sound out of tune. Now you should be in the same key as the original recording. You can keep playing the same chord shapes as before, but now you're at the same pitch as the recording.

People often use capos to raise the pitch of the guitar so that they can play in the same key as someone else. Even if you're playing on your own, you might find that changing the key makes it more comfortable for you to sing along.

Depending on the type of guitar you have and what capo you're using, you might find there's a practical limit to the number of frets you can raise the pitch by—some guitars aren't really designed to accommodate a capo after about the 8th or 9th fret. Also, the higher up the capo is placed, the more the overall tone of the guitar changes. It can sound a bit like a toy if the capo is too high, but using a capo up to about the 7th fret should sound great and be easy enough to work with.

If you'd like to try playing some of the songs in this book in their original key, here's a list showing where to place the capo. Where "0" is written, that means the song is already in the right key and doesn't need a capo. The original key of a few of the songs are slightly lower than we've written them, so a capo won't help you. (That's why not all of the songs are included in the list below.)

Capoed Fret	Song
0	When You Say Nothing At All (Ronan Keating version)
0	The First Cut Is the Deepest (Cat Stevens version)
0	No Particular Place to Go
0	Sweet Home Alabama
0	Love Me Do
0	Leaving on a Jet Plane
2	Three Little Birds
2	Chasing Cars
3	I Have a Dream
3	Coat of Many Colors
4	The Tide Is High (Blondie version)
5	The First Cut Is the Deepest (Rod Stewart version)
6	All Apologies
6	Used to Love Her
6	I Still Haven't Found What I'm Looking For
7	The First Cut Is the Deepest (Sheryl Crow version)
7	What I've Got
7	Blowin' in the Wind

BLOWIN' IN THE WIND

We'll wrap things up with Bob Dylan's seminal song from the American folk-music revival—and to do it justice, you'll need a capo.

This song was actually recorded using a capo at the 7th fret and played using exactly these chords. This combination of chords and capo will make it sound as authentic as possible.

In terms of accompaniment style, you can play a pick-strum pattern much as Dylan did on the original. It'll help to give the song some rhythmic structure, and if you also alternate the bass, a bit of interest too. Review the alternating bass patterns for each chord.

G

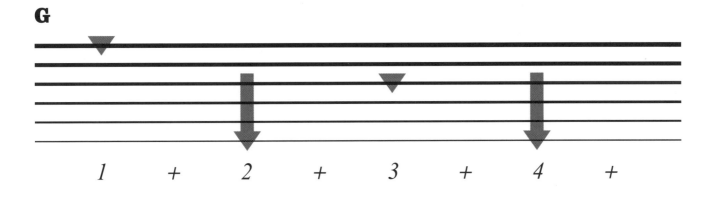

C

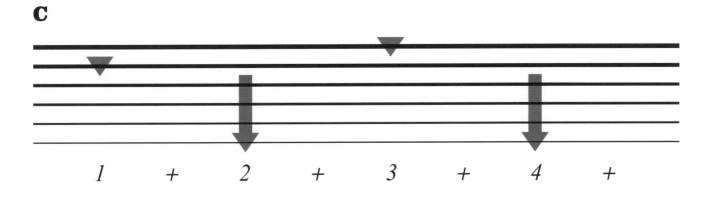

D

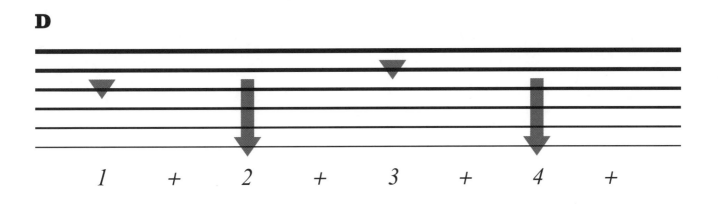

Capo: 7th fret

Verse

G   C   D   G

1. How man-y roads   must a man   walk down   be -
2. How man-y times   must a man   look up   be -

C   G

fore   you call   him a man?
fore   he can see   the sky?   Yes, and how

C   D   G

How   man - y seas   must a white   dove sail   be -
man - y ears   must one   man have   be - fore

C   D

fore   she sleeps   in   the sand?   Yes, and how
he can hear   peo - ple   cry?   Yes, and how

G   C   D   G

man - y times   must the can - non-balls   fly   be -
man - y deaths   will it take   'til he knows   that

C   G

fore   they're for - ev - er banned?
too   man - y peo - ple have died?   The

Chorus

C   D   G   C

an - swer, my friend,   is blow - in' in   the wind,   the

D   G

an - swer is blow - in' in   the wind.

Words and Music by Bob Dylan
Copyright © 1962 Warner Bros. Inc.
Copyright Renewed 1990 Special Rider Music
International Copyright Secured All Rights Reserved

FIRST 50

The First 50 series steers new players in the right direction. These books contain easy to intermediate arrangements for must-know songs. Each arrangement is simple and streamlined, yet still captures the essence of the tune.

First 50 Blues Songs You Should Play on Guitar

All Your Love (I Miss Loving) • Bad to the Bone • Born Under a Bad Sign • Dust My Broom • Hoodoo Man Blues • I'm Your Hoochie Coochie Man • Killing Floor • Little Red Rooster • Love Struck Baby • Pride and Joy • Smoking Gun • Still Got the Blues • The Thrill Is Gone • Tuff Enuff • You Shook Me • and many more.

00235790 Guitar..........................**$14.99**

First 50 Christmas Carols You Should Play on Guitar

Angels We Have Heard on High • Away in a Manger • Coventry Carol • The First Noel • God Rest Ye Merry, Gentlemen • Good King Wenceslas • The Holly and the Ivy • Jingle Bells • O Christmas Tree • O Come, All Ye Faithful • Silent Night • The Twelve Days of Christmas • Up on the Housetop • We Wish You a Merry Christmas • What Child Is This? • and more.

00236224 Guitar..........................**$12.99**

First 50 Christmas Songs You Should Play on Guitar

All I Want for Christmas Is My Two Front Teeth • Blue Christmas • The Christmas Song (Chestnuts Roasting on an Open Fire) • Do You Want to Build a Snowman? • Feliz Navidad • Happy Xmas (War Is Over) • I'll Be Home for Christmas • Mary, Did You Know? • Rudolph the Red-Nosed Reindeer • Santa Baby • Silent Night • White Christmas • Winter Wonderland • and more.

00147009 Guitar..........................**$14.99**

First 50 Classical Pieces You Should Play on Guitar

This collection includes compositions by J.S. Bach, Augustin Barrios, Matteo Carcassi, Domenico Scarlatti, Fernando Sor, Francisco Tárrega, Robert de Visée, Antonio Vivaldi and many more.

00155414 Solo Guitar................**$14.99**

First 50 Folk Songs You Should Play on Guitar

Amazing Grace • Down by the Riverside • Home on the Range • I've Been Working on the Railroad • Kumbaya • Man of Constant Sorrow • Nobody Knows the Trouble I've Seen • Oh! Susanna • She'll Be Comin' 'Round the Mountain • This Little Light of Mine • When the Saints Go Marching In • The Yellow Rose of Texas • and more.

00235868 Guitar..........................**$14.99**

First 50 Jazz Standards You Should Play on Guitar

All the Things You Are • Body and Soul • Don't Get Around Much Anymore • Fly Me to the Moon (In Other Words) • The Girl from Ipanema (Garota De Ipanema) • I Got Rhythm • Laura • Misty • Night and Day • Satin Doll • Summertime • When I Fall in Love • and more.

00198594 Solo Guitar................**$14.99**

First 50 Rock Songs You Should Play on Electric Guitar

All Along the Watchtower • Beat It • Born to Be Wild • Brown Eyed Girl • Cocaine • Detroit Rock City • Hallelujah • (I Can't Get No) Satisfaction • Iron Man • Oh, Pretty Woman • Pride and Joy • Seven Nation Army • Should I Stay or Should I Go • Smells like Teen Spirit • Smoke on the Water • When I Come Around • Wild Thing • You Really Got Me • and more.

00131159 Guitar..........................**$14.99**

First 50 Songs You Should Fingerpick on Guitar

Annie's Song • Blackbird • The Boxer • Classical Gas • Dust in the Wind • Fire and Rain • Greensleeves • Hell Hound on My Trail • Is There Anybody Out There? • Julia • Puff the Magic Dragon • Road Trippin' • Shape of My Heart • Tears in Heaven • Time in a Bottle • Vincent (Starry Starry Night) • The Wind • and more.

00149269 Solo Guitar................**$14.99**

First 50 Songs You Should Play on Acoustic Guitar

Against the Wind • Barely Breathing • Boulevard of Broken Dreams • Champagne Supernova • Crazy Little Thing Called Love • Every Rose Has Its Thorn • Fast Car • Free Fallin' • Ho Hey • I Won't Give Up • Layla • Let Her Go • Mean • One • Ring of Fire • Signs • Stairway to Heaven • Trouble • Wagon Wheel • Wish You Were Here • Yellow • Yesterday • and more.

00131209 Guitar..........................**$14.99**

First 50 Songs You Should Strum on Guitar

American Pie • Blowin' in the Wind • Daughter • Good Riddance (Time of Your Life) • Hey, Soul Sister • Home • I Will Wait • Losing My Religion • Mrs. Robinson • No Woman No Cry • Peaceful Easy Feeling • Rocky Mountain High • Sweet Caroline • Teardrops on My Guitar • Wonderful Tonight • You're Still the One • and more.

00148996 Guitar..........................**$14.99**

Prices, content and availability subject to change without notice.

www.halleonard.com

STRUM & SING

Lyrics, chord symbols, and guitar chord diagrams for your favorite songs.

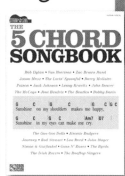

GUITAR

ACOUSTIC CLASSICS
00191891 .... $14.99

ADELE
00159855 .... $12.99

SARA BAREILLES
00102354 .... $12.99

THE BEATLES
00172234 .... $16.99

BLUES
00159335 .... $12.99

ZAC BROWN BAND
02501620 .... $14.99

COLBIE CAILLAT
02501725 .... $14.99

CAMPFIRE FOLK SONGS
02500686 .... $14.99

CHART HITS OF 2014-2015
00142554 .... $12.99

CHART HITS OF 2015-2016
00156248 .... $12.99

BEST OF KENNY CHESNEY
00142457 .... $14.99

CHRISTMAS SONGS
00171332 .... $14.99

KELLY CLARKSON
00146384 .... $14.99

COFFEEHOUSE SONGS FOR GUITAR
00285991 .... $14.99

LEONARD COHEN
00265489 .... $14.99

JOHN DENVER COLLECTION
02500632 .... $12.99

DISNEY
00233900 .... $16.99

EAGLES
00157994 .... $12.99

EASY ACOUSTIC SONGS
00125478 .... $14.99

THE 5 CHORD SONGBOOK
02501718 .... $12.99

FOLK SONGS
02501482 .... $10.99

FOLK/ROCK FAVORITES
02501669 .... $12.99

FOUR CHORD SONGS
00249581 .... $14.99

THE 4 CHORD SONGBOOK
02501533 .... $12.99

THE 4-CHORD COUNTRY SONGBOOK
00114936 .... $15.99

THE GREATEST SHOWMAN
00278383 .... $14.99

HAMILTON
00217116 .... $14.99

JACK JOHNSON
02500858 .... $17.99

ROBERT JOHNSON
00191890 .... $12.99

CAROLE KING
00115243 .... $10.99

BEST OF GORDON LIGHTFOOT
00139393 .... $14.99

DAVE MATTHEWS BAND
02501078 .... $10.95

JOHN MAYER
02501636 .... $10.99

INGRID MICHAELSON
02501634 .... $10.99

THE MOST REQUESTED SONGS
02501748 .... $12.99

JASON MRAZ
02501452 .... $14.99

PRAISE & WORSHIP
00152381 .... $12.99

ELVIS PRESLEY
00198890 .... $12.99

QUEEN
00218578 .... $12.99

ROCK AROUND THE CLOCK
00103625 .... $12.99

ROCK BALLADS
02500872 .... $9.95

ROCKETMAN
00300469 .... $17.99

ED SHEERAN
00152016 .... $14.99

THE 6 CHORD SONGBOOK
02502277 .... $12.99

CAT STEVENS
00116827 .... $14.99

TAYLOR SWIFT
00159856 .... $12.99

THE 3 CHORD SONGBOOK
00211634 .... $10.99

TODAY'S HITS
00119301 .... $12.99

TOP CHRISTIAN HITS
00156331 .... $12.99

TOP HITS OF 2016
00194288 .... $12.99

KEITH URBAN
00118558 .... $14.99

THE WHO
00103667 .... $12.99

YESTERDAY
00301629 .... $14.99

NEIL YOUNG – GREATEST HITS
00138270 .... $14.99

UKULELE

THE BEATLES
00233899 .... $16.99

COLBIE CAILLAT
02501731 .... $10.99

COFFEEHOUSE SONGS FOR UKULELE
00138238 .... $14.99

JOHN DENVER
02501694 .... $10.99

FOLK ROCK FAVORITES FOR UKULELE
00114600 .... $12.99

THE 4-CHORD UKULELE SONGBOOK
00114331 .... $14.99

JACK JOHNSON
02501702 .... $19.99

JOHN MAYER
02501706 .... $10.99

INGRID MICHAELSON
02501741 .... $12.99

THE MOST REQUESTED SONGS
02501453 .... $14.99

JASON MRAZ
02501753 .... $14.99

SING-ALONG SONGS
02501710 .... $15.99

HAL•LEONARD®

www.halleonard.com
Visit our website to see full song lists.